HypnoDontics

A Manual for
Dentists and Hypnotists

by Beryl Comar

edited by Cheryl J Elman & Michael Schuman

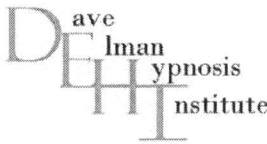

Dave Elman Hypnosis Institute

Dave Elman Hypnosis Institute Inc, Publisher

Henderson, NC 27537

Published by the
Dave Elman Hypnosis Institute, Inc
920 Barker Rd
Henderson, NC 27537
(252) 432-2205
www.DaveElmanHypnosisInstitute.com

Cover Photo: © Dragonimages | Dreamstime.com

This book is dedicated to my late husband, Dr Alexander (Sandy) Fowler MD, without whom this book would never have been written. Your words the day before you passed on gave me the courage to continue, and I heard your voice in the evenings as I wrote and wrote, and with clients as I challenged myself further.

Beryl Comar

To Rev. Timothy Jones for the foundation of this book: Thank you for your Contributions from your extensive work with hypnosis and HypnoDontics, in particular.

Beryl Comar

CONTENTS

Page

INTRODUCTION
by the Author

How this book came about

In February 2011 I was invited to participate in the UAE International Dental Conference & Arab Dental Exhibition (AEEDC Dubai 2011 February 1st -3rd). I ran a one day accredited seminar on HypnoDontics as well as a one hour talk and demonstration of hypnosis on stage. Taking a dentist from the audience, I hypnotized a volunteer to somnambulism and analgesia to demonstrate pain management following an instant induction. It was the first time most of the attendees had seen such a demonstration and the crowd that followed me out of the room wanted to know more, including where they could find a book on the subject.

I began looking for the published material and found there was little information published for dentists and, in contacting other consulting hypnotists, found that most had dealt with few dental cases. This seemed strange as Dave Elman had trained dentists in the 1960s, and his book "Hypnotherapy" had been studied and used by me for over twelve years. It was my "hypnosis bible" and I had used his techniques for countless dental clients.

I had trained with Gerald Kein, who himself was trained by Dave Elman, and widely recognized as one of the leading instructors of clinical hypnosis. It was only natural that I would turn to him for guidance and I am thankful for his generous advice in reviewing the first drafts and releasing material for inclusion.

From 1972 to 1976 I served as a teacher in Tanzania, and my dream is that this book, as an eBook, will be downloaded by dentists in poorer countries to make a difference in remote areas where those without access to expensive anesthetics and medication during dental treatment can use the natural method of hypnosis. In these areas, due to poor roads, logistics and storage including refrigeration and electricity problems, anesthetics often lose their effectiveness so, by training dentists and doctors in these hypnotic techniques painless dentistry will become more accessible to the poor around the world.

Included here is information generously given by Rev Timothy Jones from his HypnoDontics training course, as well as case studies supplied by consulting hypnotists from around the world who have already explored the world of HypnoDontics. Their contact information is added in the appendix.

Why is HypnoDontics the "untapped" field of dental practice?

No one wants to admit they would rather go shopping for shoes with their wife than go to the dentist!

It is estimated that 80% of all people are reluctant to go to the dentist. Of those 80%, they also estimate that close to half of those people put off making a dental appointment until their tooth pain is worse than they imagine the dentist will hurt.

Yet avoiding going to the dentist when something hurts in the jaw is like avoiding going to the family doctor when your stomach ache won't go away … you never know where it is going to lead, and typically it will just get worse.

This cycle of dental avoidance leads people to react anywhere from eating improperly to a fear of leaving their home. So how does this happen?

We are first imprinted with dental anxiety from the time we first teeth, which could take up to two years for all the "milk" teeth to emerge and every time we go to the dentist, or hear someone tell horror stories about their own dental visit, those anxieties come back.

Why do we call HypnoDontics the "untapped" field of dental hypnosis? Because no one wants to admit they avoid going to the dentist. However, once they are forced to seek treatment, the situation has usually worsened and the solution is unavoidably often invasive, which compounds their original fears. BUT, once the dentist sends their patient to the Consulting Hypnotist to address the patient's anxiety, the difference is immediately noticeable at chairside – both to the dentist AND the patient.

Then, once your client/patient walks out of their dentist's office wondering what the heck, they made such a fuss was for years they readily come back for more. They even brag to their friends that they saw a hypnotist, and rave about how they do not know why they did not do it sooner! Then they think, "Hey, if it was that easy, I wonder if they can help me with my …" memory, stress, big exam, speech, etc. Their friends, who will not admit they are also "scared" of going to the dentist, then call you, and word of mouth just spreads like ripples on a pond.

Once they go to a dentist trained in hypnosis, they recommend his/her skills to everyone who will listen. Dentists begin to fill their calendars with patients. THAT is why HypnoDontics is the "untapped" field of dental hypnosis! They may come to see you at first because they HAVE to, but **they come back because they WANT to.**

[8]

FOREWORD

By Dr Janet Crain

As a practicing dentist in 2003, I discovered the power of hypnosis firsthand when I was undergoing Chemotherapy for a reoccurrence of Non-Hodgkin's Lymphoma, a cancer of the lymphatic system. After my first round of chemotherapy, I lost 16 lbs., my hair fell out, my mouth was dry as a desert, and I could hardly swallow. My husband suggested I try hypnosis to control the side effects of my treatment, and with nothing to lose, I decided to take his advice. After only a 45 minute hypnotic session, I was amazed to notice my nausea disappear and my appetite return. From that day forward, I went to hypnosis two or three times a week to increase my saliva flow, to remain hungry instead of nauseous, and maintain relaxation and comfort during treatments. Over and over, the nurses and physicians remarked they had never seen anyone with the same regimen of chemotherapy need so little anti-nausea medication and maintain their weight. They never ceased to be amazed by my ability to control the side effects of my illness and the treatments.

I became a certified hypnotist with the National Guild so that I could address dental apprehension and prevent it from interfering with my patient's ability to gain control and seek oral healthcare. As alternative medicine became more and more mainstreamed, hypnosis as a medical modality continued to gain new credibility. The assertion that we must address both the mind AND body if we are to treat our patients with the highest quality oral healthcare just made sense.

According to Shawn Watson, author of an article on the subject of dental fear, an estimated 80% of adult Americans have a fear of the dentist. Though it is not our role to judge their fear, that fear prevents so many from attaining the best oral healthcare; it is our responsibility to combat this trend. If we focus on changing the dental experience and begin to address emotional as well as the physical issues, we can help more patients control their emotions and put fears to rest.

A resurgence of interest in alternative of interest in alternative therapies has led to new discoveries and research about the mind & body connection. Essentially, scientists have proven that the mind is extremely powerful and it plays a role in healing. In 1986, Dr. Earl Bakken introduced term *cyberphysiology*, which is the study of how nerve mediated autonomic responses can be modified by a learning process. Hypnosis, a cyberphysiological strategy, allows one to manage fearful thoughts. Recent research conducted on the brain supports this further. Science affirms that hypnosis gives a person the ability to control their amygdale, the area of the brain where fear is triggered. Therefore, when someone is in a hypnotic trance, the automatic "fight, flight or freeze" response, which triggers dental apprehension, is relaxed. The body and the mind consequently experience a deep state of relaxation.

Dental Apprehension is costly in time, money and emotions. It affects not only the image of dentistry, but the experience of oral health for everybody – the dentist, the staff and the patient. In her book on Dental Hypnosis, Beryl Comar has organized a comprehensive explanation and guide specifically for the dental practice. She argues the benefits of hypnosis in the dental practice, and she teaches foundational knowledge about hypnosis. Reading her book, you will learn how to address fears, anxieties, and phobias early in the dental visit. This book is informational for the dentist and hypnotist to incorporate hypnosis into the field of dentistry confidently and effectively.

Janet Crain D.M.D

Author of If you want an Eggroll get out of the Pizzeria

INTRODUCTION

From Gerald Kein,
President OmniHypnosis

When Beryl Comar sent me a copy of her new book on HypnoDontics, I thought "Oh no. Not another book on hypnosis." Then, even before I read it, I thought about Beryl. I remember when she took my advance training program over 15 years ago. I remember her excitement about learning hypnosis. I remember as she absorbed the information like a sponge. I just had a feeling that she was going to end up being one of the really great ones in our profession. As the years went by, I watched her career as she began as a fledgling hypnotist up through today when she is recognized as one of the best hypnosis instructors in the work. I am very proud of what she is done not only for herself but even more for our profession. So as I began reading the book I just had a feeling that the quality of the book would parallel the quality of her work overall in her professional career.

I was honored indeed when Beryl told me that she had incorporated several of the HypnoDontic techniques that she had learned from me over the years. As I began reading the book after a very short time I knew I had a very special book in my hands. Let's face it, writing about dental hypnosis is not exactly the most exciting plot that somebody could write a book about. That's absolutely incorrect in this book. The book not only held my attention from cover to cover but the way the material has been presented is extremely easy to read, understand and use in your professional career. My reputation in the field of honesty and integrity has been earned over many years. As you know a reputation takes a long time to build and can be lost in an instant. Because of this I rarely recommend anyone or any product unless I consider that person or that product the best of the best. I have absolutely no problem recommending this book to anyone who wants to use hypnosis in a professional career or as an adjunct to the dental profession.

The amount of information given in this book is truly amazing. It starts off with a very brief history of dentistry. It discusses the development of hypnosis is a surgical pain block as compared to chemical anesthetics, and a place of hypnosis in managed dental care today. It then moves into information for the consulting hypnotist. It details the physiological, psychological and sociological aspects affecting HypnoDontics, both from a dental practitioner's and the dental patient's point of view. The removal of dental fear, anxiety and other dental stressors are excellently covered in a great sample hypnosis session.

Beryl then goes into advice how one can use hypnosis as an everyday tool for self, staff and patients. It includes some excellent recommendations from a dentist who has become a licensed hypnotist and uses hypnosis with her patient as well as those dentists who referred patients to hypnosis and how they work together. This is great information that will help you incorporate these techniques in your office.

For me, when Beryl teaches for dentists and hypnotherapists how to work with children. I've always found this to be, for me, the most satisfying part of the work. Beryl also gives you some great scripts that you can immediately use. You also receive not only scripts but more advanced techniques for your toolbox such as regression to cause, NLP and parts therapy among others.

I think one of the most important parts of any book is giving actual case histories of how people have used the technique successfully. You will read several of them in this book and this will give you the confidence that you can do this work successfully.

Beryl states the objective of this book is to show you how easily HypnoDontics can change dental practice. It will renew approaches to helping people with easily resolved anxieties and habits, and it will invigorate your interest in this fascinating mind science... And it all starts with the most basic of uplifting human emotions... The smile - both yours and those of your "fixed" clients and patients! Beryl meets these objectives perfectly And has written one of the Best Books on HypnoDontics I have ever read.

I have been professionally involved in the field of hypnosis for over 55 years both as a therapist and as an instructor. There are many books written about hypnotism but only a few written about HypnoDontics. I am totally confident that as both the hypnotist and the dentist become aware of this book it will be considered The Bible of HypnoDontics. This is not just another boring book written by somebody who just wants to write a book to enhance his or her reputation. This is a book written by a professional for professionals covering the material needed in a logical, easy to read and easy to employ method. I am very proud of Beryl for writing this much-needed book.

They will thank you

Gerald Kein
Director: Omni Hypnosis Training Center

How this Book is Organized
This book is presented in SIX parts:

The first section is for the general reader, and examines the historic evolution of dentistry, the development of hypnosis as a surgical pain block as compared to chemical anesthetics, and the place of hypnosis in managed dental care today.

The second section is for the consulting hypnotist, and details the physiological, psychological and sociological aspects affecting HypnoDontics - both from the point of view of the dental practitioner and the dental patient. We offer suggestions on how to expand into HypnoDontics, how to approach branching into dental anxiety, either exclusively or adjunctively with an existing hypnotherapeutic practice. *"Working with the Dentist"* examines the stressors dental practitioners face on a daily basis so the Consulting Hypnotist can more empathetically structure a proposal for offering a dentist a sample session.

The third section is for the dentist, with advice on how s/he can use hypnosis as an everyday tool for self, staff and patients. It includes recommendations from a dentist who has become a licensed hypnotist and uses hypnosis with her patient as well as those dentists who have referred patients to hypnotists and how they worked together. There is information for those dentists who wish to complete accredited training in hypnosis. Lastly, we present the current role of hypnotherapy in the practice of dentistry as a complementary therapy, and our expectations for the future.

Section four is for dentists and hypnotherapists working with children. We describe the growth of teeth from infancy along with some of the concerns of tooth development in growing children. This is followed by suggestions for hypnotists and dentists to work with children along with examples and some scripts.

Our fifth section contains case histories from the authors and contributing consulting hypnotists from around the world. Their contact information can be found in the Appendix

Our sixth section contains some helpful script samples, always with the caveat that an excellent consulting hypnotist will have more advanced techniques in his or her toolbox (regression to cause, parts therapy among others)

In the Appendix the reader will find references and a bibliography, a glossary of useful vocabulary as well as a list of specialists around the world who work with hypnosis for dental clients and train certified hypnosis courses.

The objective of this book is to show you how easily HypnoDontics can change dental practice. It will renew approaches to helping people with easily resolved anxieties and habits, and it will invigorate your interest in this fascinating mind science … and it all starts with the most basic of uplifting human emotions … the smile – both yours and those of your "fixed" clients and patients!

Whether dentist, consulting hypnotist or patient - We wish you the very best in your new direction!

SECTION 1

About Hypnosis

In this chapter we explore:

1. THE HISTORY OF DENTAL HYPNOSIS
2. THE NATURE OF HYPNOSIS

1. The History of Dental Hypnosis

i. The Early History of Dentistry

Oral disease has been a people problem from the beginning of history. Skulls of Cro-Magnon peoples inhabiting the earth 25,000 years ago show evidence of tooth decay, and the earliest recorded reference to oral disease is from an ancient Sumerian text written in 5000 BC describing "tooth worms" as a cause of dental decay.

There is also historical evidence that the Chinese used acupuncture around 2700 BC to treat pain associated with tooth decay, and evidence has been found that Stone Age people in Pakistan were using dental drills made of flint around 9,000 years ago.

Despite these findings, cavities were not of much concern in an agricultural society that did not know of sugar until the 1600's. Life expectation was then only 50-60 years, gum disease was the predominant concern.

Much of early dentistry was practiced as part of the general practice of medicine and throughout the Middle Ages in Europe, dentistry was provided to wealthier individuals by physicians or surgeons who went to the patient's home. For the working class, dentistry took place in the marketplace, where self-taught individuals would extract teeth for a fee.

From the Middle Ages to the early 1700s, most dentistry was provided by so-called "barber surgeons." These jacks-of-all-trades would not only extract teeth and perform minor surgery, but they also cut hair, applied leeches to let blood, and performed embalming.

In the 1770's, two popular books, "*Natural History of Human Teeth*" (1771), and "*Practical Treatise on the Diseases of the Teeth*" (1778), were written by English physiologist John Hunter, surgeon general to the British army, which began the slow separation of dentistry proper from medicine.

Pain Control

For the privileged, there was no real difference between medical and dental practitioners and for them, dental pain was commonly treated using natural herbs as a pain block up to about 1660. At that time, a mixture of opium and alcohol (laudanum) became the standard until the mid-1800's, when cocaine became medically popular before the introduction of ether and other inhalation drugs in 1844.

For most of the working class though, pain supplements were prohibitively expensive and as dental work was so painful, those "patients" were either held down while "operated" on, knocked unconscious, or offered a couple of swigs of strong spirits to dull their senses.

As an interesting side-note to the recently re-popularized "Instant Induction" techniques, there is historical record of a wandering Portuguese monk, the Abbe Faria, appearing in Paris in 1815. His experiences in India and the Far East had taught him to produce the somnambulistic trance simply by gazing steadily at the patient and then suddenly shouting, 'Sleep!' Despite many wonderful cures, Faria was labeled a charlatan, but he was one of the first to proclaim the cause of the trance state rested within the patient, and was not due to any magnetic influence of the operator.

At the same time in history, mesmerism was making great strides in France and many operations were performed under its influence. In one of the first recorded procedures using mesmerism for dentistry, in 1836, it was reported that Dr. Jean-Victor Oudet, a Parisian physician, removed a tooth using what is now called hypnoanethesia, as the word hypnosis was not in use at the time.

Dr. John Elliotson

One of the most steadfast mesmerists engaged in this work was the Baron du Potet. In 1837 he visited London to provide demonstrations to the public, and he attracted the attention of Dr. John Elliotson, the man who introduced the stethoscope into England and considered one of the most brilliant men in the history of English medicine.

As the story goes, Dr. Elliotson, a skeptic, was almost dragged along to one of du Potet's demonstrations by an associate and, convinced of chicanery, returned the next week to another demonstration with two other physicians, one an eye specialist. At one point, Elliotson and his two associates, apparently uninvited, mounted the stage when du Potet's female subject was in state. The doctor opened her eyes to examine them and, after searching studiously in both eyes for reflex action, declared the lady to be in trance.

Not a man given to suffering fools gladly, it was said Dr. Elliotson then inserted a needle into one of her fingers. Receiving no response, he repeated the action with another finger and again found no response. He began to realize the importance of this new method of treatment and he began to experiment with 'magnetic sleep' in his University College Hospital.

He was soon able to prove its value in the treatment of nervous disorders, as well as certain other medical cases. While the use of hypnosis as an anesthetic could not be disputed, he quickly aroused the envy and jealousy of the medical profession and in 1838, the University Council passed a resolution forbidding the use of mesmerism in the hospital.

Elliotson immediately resigned. He said to the Dean of the University who tried to persuade him to give up mesmerism in order to retain his position in the hospital: 'The Institution (University) was established for the discovery and dissemination of truth. All other considerations are secondary. We should lead the public, not the public us. The sole question is whether the matter is the truth or not.'

Elliotson continued to use mesmerism with much success in spite of bitter opposition and despite his detractors. He was regarded as such an outstanding physician that the Royal College of Physicians invited him to deliver the Harveian oration in 1846.

The Harveian Oration is a yearly lecture held at the Royal College of Physicians of London encouraging practitioners to seek out and prove new treatments. In 1656 William Harvey, the discoverer of systemic circulation, instituted this custom and made financial provision for the college to hold an annual feast on St. Lukes Day (October 18). At this event, an oration would be delivered to praise the college's benefactors and "to exhort the Fellows and Members of this college to search for and study the secrets of nature by way of experiment."

Elliotson accepted the offer to speak and chose to defend mesmerism. He went on to found the Mesmeric Hospital in London, with similar institutions soon established in other big cities such as Edinburgh and Dublin. From one of these, in Exeter, it was reported that Dr. Parker, a surgeon, performed over 200 successful operations under mesmerism.

Dr. James Braid

Meanwhile, Lafontaine, a Swiss magnetizer touring England giving exhibitions, brought the subject to the notice of Dr. James Braid of Manchester, who was destined to bring a breath of scientific reason to bear upon the controversial subject. Dr James Braid is today regarded by many as the 'Father of (Modern) Hypnosis', and coined the term "hypnosis" – by mistake.

At first Braid's technique was to hold a small bright object between 8 to 16 inches (20cm-40cm) in front of his subjects' eyes so the eyes became strained, after which the eyelids would often close spontaneously. As he continued with his experiments however he found he achieved trance states by suggestions alone.

In 1842, having concluded the phenomena was a form of sleep, Dr Braid named the phenomena after Hypnos, the Greek god of sleep and master of dreams. By 1847 however, he had discovered that all the major phenomena of hypnotism such as catalepsy, anesthesia and amnesia, could be induced without sleep.

Realizing his choice of the term hypnosis had been a mistake; he tried to rename it to Monoideism, but it was too late as his terms of "Hypnosis" and "Hypnotism" had already become widely adopted as part of all the major European languages.

In a defining number of papers arising from his studies, Dr. Braid established that hypnotism was not due to any mesmerism or magnetism, and echoed the words of Abbe Faria some two decades earlier that the cause of trance rested within the patient and was not due to any magnetic influence.

Braid proved the point scientifically by the medical standards of the day, and concluded that hypnosis is *"reconcilable with well-known physiological and psychological principles."*

Dr. James Esdaile

Around the same time in India, Dr. James Esdaile, a young Scottish surgeon, began to successfully experiment with mesmerism after reading Elliotson's work. In 1846, a Government Committee reported favorably on his work and placed him in charge of a special hospital in Calcutta where Esdaile performed several thousand minor and nearly three hundred major operations under mesmerism.

Incredible for the times, Esdaile was able to reduce the operative death rate from 40-50% to only 5% by the use of mesmerism. But, yet again, traditionalists in the establishment *(the Calcutta Medical College)* did their best to discredit him and put out the story that his patients, who had undergone the most severe operations without pain, were a 'set of hardened and determined impostors'.

However, Esdaile had the last laugh, as the local newspapers which had first condemned him, changed their opinions on seeing case after case of successful and painless surgery. They then turned indignantly on those members of the orthodox medical profession who had tried to mislead them.

ii. Hypnosis, Chemical Anesthesia and Dentistry

Esdaile, like Elliotson before him, hoped mesmerism would become widely available for the benefit of the public during medical and dental procedures. This was not to be. In his 1846 book *"Mesmerism in India, and its Practical Application in Surgery and Medicine"*, Esdaile wrote that he feared … *"that not many of this generation will live to benefit by Mesmerism, if they wait till it is admitted into the Pharmacopoeia"* (p. 9).

Two years earlier in 1844, Dr. Horace Wells, a Connecticut dentist, initiated the use of nitrous oxide (laughing gas) inhalation during dental therapy and founded the concept of inhalation analgesia and anesthesia. On October 18, 1846, less than six months after Esdaile's book went to press, the dentist William T.G. Morton applied an ether-soaked sponge to the patient Gilbert Abbott. The surgeon, John Collins Warren, who had experimented unsuccessfully with mesmeric anesthesia earlier in his career, removed a tumor from Abbott's neck without the patient showing any signs of pain.

Within two years, ether, nitrous oxide, chloroform, and other chemical anesthetics were widely used in surgery and the international medical community, more comfortable with a measurable science, quickly adopted inhalation anesthesia as a standard surgical management procedure. The forward thrust of hypnotism and hypnotherapy was again shuffled off to the sidelines.

Seven years before that, in 1839, two American dentists, Horace H. Hayden and Chapin A. Harris, founded the Baltimore College of Dental Surgery in North America. This raised the standard of dental training, curriculum and exams. With the founding of the college, dentistry became an autonomous profession in the USA before it had emerged as such in Europe, and dentistry came of age and matured into Dental Art and Science in 1900.

Yet a pain block was still needed. The first local aesthetic was Cocaine (isolated from coca leaves), initiated in the 1860s, but it came into common clinical usage in 1884. By the turn of the twentieth century, though the addictive properties of cocaine had become clear and it had become obvious that while the anesthetic characteristics of cocaine were desirable, the euphoria and subsequent addiction it produced were not.

With the onset of the Age of Industrialization in North America, it was a time of tremendous scientific progress, and the new discipline of organic chemistry enabled the synthesis of the first analog of cocaine in 1905.

The first synthetic local anesthetic was Procaine, better remembered today by its trade name Novocain, but it too was not without its problems. It took a very long time to set (i.e. to produce the desired anesthetic result), wore off too quickly, and was not nearly as potent as cocaine. On top of that, Novocain is classified as an ester, which has a very high potential to cause allergic reactions. It was estimated that about one in 100 persons who received it developed at least minor allergic reactions to it.

Faced with the legal and ethical difficulties associated with the use of cocaine as a local anesthetic, and with the inefficiencies and allergic reactions associated with the use of Procaine, it is not surprising that many dentists of the day worked without any local anesthetic at all, even though nitrous oxide gas was available. In third world countries, that is still the case today.

The first modern local anesthetic agent was Lidocaine, invented in the 1940's. Prior to its introduction, nitrous oxide and Procaine were the major sources of pain relief during dental procedures. Lidocaine though proved to be so successful that during the 1940's and 1950's, the use of Procaine and nitrous oxide gas as primary anesthetic agents all but vanished. Today, nitrous oxide is used principally as an anti-anxiety in palliative care, and Novocaine is no longer available.

Lidocaine (along with all other injectable anesthetics used in modern dentistry) is in a broad class of chemicals called amides, and unlike ester-based anesthetics, amides are hypoallergenic. It sets quickly and when combined with a small amount of epinephrine (adrenalin), it produces profound anesthesia for several hours. As a result, Lidocaine is still the most widely applied local anesthetic in use for general dentistry today.

iii. Tooth Cavity Rates Before 1900

It took until the 1900's for the practice of dentistry to be recognized as a distinct profession from medicine. Tooth decay (dental caries) was not a major problem before 1886, which was the year the first sugar-saturated mass-marketed soft drink, Coca Cola, was invented. Prior to the trend toward soft drinks, people only tended to eat sweet foods at meal times. In a primarily agricultural society, meals were high in fat but fairly low in sugar, and the closest most people got to sugar during the course of a week was a slice of pie or cake.

Although sugar first came to the attention of the Europeans in the early 1500's after the new world was discovered, it was expensive in Europe and only the wealthy could afford it. As an example, Queen Elizabeth I was famous for her black teeth *(Elizabethi.org)*. An interesting historical anecdote is that Queen Elizabeth 1 suffered for a long while from a severe toothache but was too afraid to have her tooth extracted. One of her Archbishops offered to have one of his own extracted to show her that the procedure was rather simple.

After seeing that the Archbishop could tolerate the pain of the extraction, she agreed to have her own troublesome tooth removed, but not before she asked the loyal Archbishop to go through the painful procedure again by having a second tooth extracted so the Queen was satisfied that it was safe! The rest of her subjects worked the land and, as oral hygiene was nearly non-existent, tended to lose teeth primarily to gum disease, not tooth decay.

When developing a treatment plan, the HypnoDontic Practitioner should be aware that almost everyone who is prone to caries has a specific habit in which one form of sugar or another soaks the teeth many times a day *(double-double coffee, sweetened gum, pop, etc.).*

These sugar habits are estimated to account for up to 95% of all caries, and the Consulting Hypnotist should attempt to discover those habits during their intake interviews as once the habit is identified, we can hypnotherapeutically suggest substituting a non-sugared drink or food in its place. As a matter of fact, dental science knows that if there were no fermentable sugars in our diets we would not develop cavities, even if we never brushed our teeth.

2. THE NATURE OF HYPNOSIS

Hypnosis is far more understood today, although not entirely. It is accepted as an altered state of consciousness which has nothing to do with sleep. During a hypnotic induction, there is suspension of both reality testing and critical analysis. In recent years there is an increasing amount of evidence to support the view that hypnosis is a state of altered brain function (using measurements of cortical evoked potentials and EEC studies). There is also supporting evidence from functional brain imaging procedures such as PUI scans.

During hypnosis it has been shown that hypnotized individuals switch from left hemisphere activation to right hemisphere activation. The left cortex deals with logical, critical, appraisal functions whereas the right cortex is more involved with emotional functions, feelings, imagination, creativity and both musical and art appreciation.

It is important to realize that hypnosis is a natural state and that all hypnosis is essentially self-hypnosis and is a consent state. The role of the hypnotherapist is to teach patients to enter this state at will and to be able to use autohypnosis as a self-help therapy. Providing people with one or two simple examples helps to overcome the very negative images that may result from watching stage hypnosis performances.

We are all aware of times when we have driven a car over a familiar route and have arrived at our destination with no memory of the journey because we have been involved with internal thoughts. If however, an unusual incident had occurred during such a journey then full attention would have returned instantly.

The film ET provides another good example of how our brain processes affect our emotional state. When first shown in cinemas large numbers of the audience ended up in tears. Ones left brain is fully aware that we are watching a film about a model made of bits of wire and plastic, but our right brain says "yes, but he is dying" and we cry.

Hypnosis is not merely a complementary therapy. This ability of patients to enter the hypnotic state can augment conventional therapies but not necessarily replace them. One of the major advantages of the use of hypnosis is that treatment is usually quick compared to conventional psychological techniques. For example behavioral therapy, while effective, is very time consuming. Treatment of phobias such as severe dental phobia may take several weeks or even months to treat conventionally, whereas a solution with hypnosis may only require two to three visits. Self-hypnosis used at home is a useful element, a learned technique it requires persistence but once learned, it is a "tool for life".

i. Hypnosis Definitions

Hypnosis is not something one person "does" to another. Actually all hypnosis is self-hypnosis because it is the *client* who uses his or her abilities, including concentration and imagination, to produce what we recognize as "hypnotic" effects.

Among practitioners the most common view of hypnosis is that it is an altered state of consciousness; your awareness differs somehow to your everyday sense of reality. This is often referred to as being in a trance. However, for many, perhaps most people, being in hypnosis does not seem much different from how they feel at other times.

One difference such people usually notice is that they feel relaxed. Often they feel more deeply relaxed than they have ever felt before. This has led to claims that hypnosis is nothing more than profound relaxation. Yet laboratory tests prove hypnosis is something more than relaxation: e.g., after hypnosis the heart rate remains slower longer than after relaxation alone.

Another definition holds that hypnosis is a heightened state of suggestibility. What does this mean? Does it mean that people in hypnosis will accept suggestions more readily than people not in hypnosis? That does not explain anything. People are readily suggestible without hypnosis -- the mammoth advertising industry attests to that -- and people in hypnosis by definition want to cooperate. Of course, they accept suggestions. They suspend their disbelief as they would while reading a novel. Yet suggest something that is distasteful to them and they will quickly stop cooperating -- just as they would drop a novel which offended them.

Definition of Hypnosis (National Guild of Hypnotists): *Hypnosis is the bypass of the critical factor of the conscious mind and the acceptance of selective thinking in the subconscious. A state of mind, enhanced by (although not exclusively) mental and physical relaxation, in which our subconscious is able to communicate with our conscious mind.*

It is usually easier to define "hypnosis" by what it does rather than what it is. Additionally, it is widely accepted as a most excellent process for accessing our inner potential. The state of mind referred to may be brought about either unaided by oneself (self-hypnosis) or with the help of another person. If this other person is a trained professional, who utilises the resultant state of mind to encourage beneficial change to occur, the process is referred to as "*Hypnotherapy*".

ii. Common Myths About Hypnosis

- **I will lose consciousness and be like a zombie:** That is false. Consciousness is heightened during hypnosis. You will be even more aware of what is going on. Your hearing will improve while in hypnosis. Your thinking will be clearer. Your body may appear to be asleep, but your mind will be much more alert than normal. Imagination, concentration and memory all dramatically improve while in hypnosis.

- **I can get stuck in trance:** There is no possibility of being stuck in trance. You can however drift into sleep if left with no further suggestions, but you would wake from that sleep naturally, feeling perfectly OK.

- **I won't remember what happened:** Actually most people do remember what happens during trance, unless the therapist gives them the suggestion for them not to remember. There can be many reasons why the therapist might use this suggestion to stop the conscious mind from remembering. A traumatic experience could be a prime example).

- **I will tell all my dark secrets:** People can lie in hypnosis. The subconscious mind will always protect us.

- **I can open my eyes so I am not hypnotized:** Eyes do not have to be closed for you to be in trance. Children are a good example of this. Watch them while they are watching a cartoon and notice their eyes are wide open, but their mind is elsewhere. They are in a natural trance and possibly in the cartoon.

- **The hypnotist will control me**. False. The client is always in control and always decides whether to cooperate with suggestions. Any suggestion that violates any strongly held feeling, moral, ethical or religious belief will be automatically rejected by both your conscious mind and your unconscious mind.

- **Hypnotherapists swing pendulums to put you into trance:** This myth was perpetuated in Hollywood when the hypnotist would swing a pendulum in front of the subject's face. You can use a pendulum but why do so when there are faster, easier and more modern methods? All a good hypnotist does is to just talk. Hypnotherapists may use pendulums to communicate with the unconscious mind however, the pendulums sole purpose being is to magnify minute subconscious muscle movements.

The truth is what a client says about Trance:

".....felt like I was in a warm cocoon" "lovely....(like) immersing myself in a warm bath, total relaxation" "like being in a vacuum and nothing was required of me but to just relax...." "... like a mental massage... and I know it will last much longer than any body massage...."

Hypnosis is safe

Hypnosis is fun

Hypnosis can change your life

Section 2

For the Consulting Hypnotist

In this section, we shall be looking at:

1. BACKGROUND INFORMATION ON ADULT DENTAL HEALTH

2. DENTAL ANXIETY

3. OTHER ISSUES

4. WORKING WITH THE DENTIST

5. HOW TO EXPAND INTO THE WORLD OF HYPNODONTICS

6. STRUCTURING THE CLIENT APPOINTMENT - STEPS

Note: the Dental Practitioner is the expert, and the Consulting Hypnotist is prohibited by professional standards from suggesting a client take, or cease taking, any sort of medication, whether over-the-counter or not. Those recommendations are the exclusive domain of health care professionals.

We are not aiming here to teach anyone to be a hypnotherapist; we recommend training in Basic to Advanced hypnosis before advancing into HypnoDontics. Some approved training centers are listed in the appendix.

1. BACKGROUND INFORMATION ON ADULT DENTAL HEALTH

This section contains information for the Consulting Hypnotist so s/he may have a deeper understanding of client's dental issues, if they arise. Hypnotherapists must choose their phrasing carefully when dealing with dental patients, in the event the client has not disclosed experiencing allergic dental reactions, in order to avoid stimulating a remembered physical reaction, like anaphylaxis, while in-state.

It is crucial that client intake information be issue-specific to avoid giving rise to negative physical abreactions in the more responsive client.

The Impact of Poor Oral Health on Overall Health

Oral health is not only important to our appearance and sense of well-being, but also to overall health. Cavities and gum disease may contribute to many serious conditions, including heart disease, diabetes, respiratory diseases, and premature and low weight babies. Untreated cavities can also be painful and lead to serious infections.

Maintaining good oral health includes keeping teeth free from cavities and preventing gum disease. Poor oral health can affect appearance and self-esteem. It has been linked to sleeping problems, as well as behavioral and developmental problems in children. Poor oral health can also affect the ability to chew and digest food properly, and good nutrition itself is important to helping build strong teeth and gums that can resist disease and promote healing.

Smoking is a major risk factor for oral and dental disease as tobacco reduces blood flow to the gums; therefore, the gums do not get the oxygen and nutrients needed to stay healthy and prevent bacterial infection.

The Risks of Poor Gum Health

Gum disease resulting in an inflammation of the gums, may also affect the bone supporting the teeth. Plaque is a sticky colorless film of bacteria that constantly builds up, thickens and hardens on the teeth. If daily brushing and flossing do not remove plaque, it can harden into tartar and contribute to infections in the gums.

Left untreated, gum disease can lead to the loss of teeth and an increased risk of complicating more serious diseases, including heart disease and stroke. The bacteria in plaque can travel from the mouth into the bloodstream. It has been linked to the clogging of arteries and damage to heart valves. The same bacteria can also travel to the lungs, causing infection or aggravate existing lung conditions.

Additionally, poor dental health can chronically negatively engage the immune system, drawing required resources from on-going whole body revitalization.

Adverse Effects of Local Anesthetics

In their 2001 manual *"Local Anesthesia in Dentistry,"* Drs. Rainer Rahn & Benedikt Ball of Germany indicated local anesthetics and vasoconstrictor agents may cause adverse effects in patients suffering from various diseases. They concluded that local anesthetic drugs may lead to adverse effects in patients suffering from convulsive disorders, in pregnant women, in children, and in aging patients.

They also noted that anesthetics with epinephrine may be dangerous to patients with cardiovascular diseases, especially those with heart failure, angina pectoris, myocardial infarction, cardiac arrhythmias and hypertension. We note that in these patients, a complementary hypnotherapeutic solution allowing for a smaller dosage may well be of interest to the dental practitioner.

Allergic Reactions

The signs and symptoms of allergic reaction include:

- generalized body rash or skin redness
- itching, urticaria (hives)
- bronchospasm (difficulty breathing)
- swelling of the throat
- asthma
- abdominal cramping
- irregular heartbeat
- hypotension (low blood pressure)
- swelling of the face and lips (angioneurotic edema)

Allergic reactions can have any degree of severity ranging from minor itching to full-blown anaphylaxis. In a very serious anaphylactic reaction, the patient may experience serious difficulty breathing due to restriction of the bronchioles in the lungs, or swelling in the throat area due to Urticaria *(a specific type of skin rash where there is a release of inflammatory mediators)* as well as seriously low blood pressure leading to anaphylactic shock. This set of events, left untreated, can lead to death.

First Aid Information for the Consulting Hypnotist

Fortunately, the majority of allergic reactions to local anesthetics is fairly mild and is easily treated with light antihistamines like Benadryl. In the vast majority of situations, patients who have patch-tested allergic to all modern local anesthetics can be safely injected for necessary dental work using an anesthetic without vasoconstrictor, provided the dentist is ready with the appropriate drugs and training necessary to combat reactions that could include anaphylactic reaction.

As the most frequent problem encountered in anaphylactic shock is swelling in the neck area that can block breathing, this is the first aid protocol (JAMA);

1. Position the client on his or her back with the feet elevated.

2. Maintain an airway using the chin lift-head tilt method. In most cases, this is the only measure needed to see the patient through the emergency. If the patient is breathing on his or her own, then the next steps in the emergency protocol will be unnecessary.

3. If the patient is not breathing on their own, employ rescue breathing and proceed to the next steps in the emergency protocol (the ABC's of first aid)

4. Check the carotid artery for heartbeat and use chest compressions if necessary.

5. Definitive care includes Defibrillation if necessary if an AED (Automatic External Defibrillator) is available.

Information About Nitrous Oxide

A Canadian Periodontist, considering HypnoDontics for his anxious patients, told a hypnotist that rather than referring patients out for anxiety therapy, he preferred to use Nitrous Oxide (N_2O). Nitrous Oxide is still very much in use today and dentists regularly advertise it to attract patients who may not otherwise consider needed dental work – AND--, it has also been demonstrated to increase suggestibility and imaginative ability.

Specifically, researchers in Britain tested 30 volunteers, on two occasions, for dental surgery during a suggestibility testing study. During one visit, volunteers inhaled 25% nitrous oxide, the other time they inhaled normal air/oxygen.

During each visit, the volunteers were given a standardized test of suggestibility and a test to measure imaginative ability. They were not inducted into an entrained state. Participants were also asked about whether they expected the drug to affect their suggestibility. They then found that nitrous oxide increased suggestibility and imaginative ability by about 10%.

When asked in which session they thought they had received the drug, volunteers were not very accurate at identifying the correct session. From the results of testing after administration of the two gasses, researchers drew the conclusions that the noted increase in suggestibility was a real drug effect and not just a boost caused by positive expectations.

Researchers also hypothesized that it might be possible to boost suggestibility even further with a higher dose, and indicated that adding a hypnotic induction could boost suggestibility still further.

The actual mechanism of action of N_2O is still unknown (it appears that there are quite a few different mechanisms at work)! However, it has been observed that N_2O depresses almost all forms of sensation – especially hearing, touch and pain, and seems to inhibit some emotional centers in the brain, although the ability to concentrate or perform intelligent acts is only minimally affected, as is memory.

Interestingly, inhalation sedation has also been found to be very effective in eliminating, or at least minimizing, severe gagging.

How does pregnancy affect dental health?

During pregnancy, many women experience increased sensitivity and puffiness of the gums. Pregnancy causes an alteration in the estrogen and progesterone levels that, when coupled with plaque that is present in the mouth, can cause an exaggerated form of gingivitis (inflammation of the gums). Professional dental cleanings twice during one's pregnancy, as well as frequent daily brushing (3 times a day) and flossing will greatly reduce gum swelling and sensitivity.

Most dental treatment can be safely completed during pregnancy. Despite the extremely low radiation of dental x-rays, routine check-up x-rays are usually avoided during pregnancy if the expectant mother has received routine dental care, and is in good dental health. If the expectant mother is in pain, dental x-rays can be safely taken, but I advise using two lead aprons to shield the radiation. Dental anesthetics at regular doses, some types of antibiotics and pain medication are not harmful during pregnancy.

How does diet affect the development of cavities?

Dental cavities are an infection caused by a combination of carbohydrate-containing foods and bacteria that live in our mouths. The bacteria are contained in a film that continuously forms on and around our teeth. We call this film plaque. Although there are many different types of bacteria in our mouths, only a few are associated with cavities. When these bacteria find carbohydrates, they digest them and produce acid. As "surgery foods" (candy, sugar frosted breakfast cereals, ice cream, soda, Kool-Aid, etc.) and other carbohydrates are eaten, the acid begins to dissolve the hard enamel that forms the outer coating of our teeth. Every exposure to these foods allows an acid attack on the teeth for about twenty minutes!

Q: How can I make better food choices to prevent tooth decay?

> **A:** Both diet and oral hygiene impacts the rate of tooth decay. Foods most likely to promote cavities are sticky candy and fruits like raisins. Certain beverages can also damage teeth like soda (both regular and diet) and some sports drinks. Certain foods can have a positive effect on oral health like apples, yogurt, and cheese.
>
> To prevent tooth decay, brush after every meal and before going to bed with a fluoride containing toothpaste. See your dentist regularly for examinations and professional cleanings.

Q: If I have experienced abuse in the past, will I be afraid of the dentist?

> **A:** One of the most common reasons that people fear the dentist is because they had a dentist cause them physical pain during treatment, and then criticized them when they complained. Dentists who practice this way do cause their patients emotional trauma that could be considered abuse. I suggest you find a compassionate dentist who has a good reputation with treating fearful patients. Ask friends or family members whom they recommend. See a qualified hypnotist, hypnotherapist or dentist to help alleviate the fear(s).

2. DENTAL ANXIETY

Some patients are so dental phobic that they avoid dental care at all costs and may sometimes require sedation or general anesthesia (being put to sleep) to have their dental treatment completed. Dentists do not like or want to do this and view Sedation and general anesthesia as a last resort for most patients seeking general dental treatment.

There are many reasons for dental anxiety with many recalling a past traumatic experience during a dental visit, and others fear being confronted by a dentist about the condition of their mouths. Unhelpful dental stories from family, peers, news and in advertisements can compound their fear and anxiety. There are some parents who threaten their children with a trip to the dentist if they do not behave so no wonder they avoid such visits in the future!

Anxious patients will often schedule, then cancel appointments or not turn up on the day because they "just can't get there". They may abuse over-the-counter medications or use distractions to avoid dental treatment which puts them at risk for serious dental infections. They may suffer from low self-esteem due to the appearance of their teeth.

Nowadays dentists can use powerful local anesthetics, air abrasion, nitrous oxide (laughing gas), relaxation techniques, and many other methods to help a patient overcome their fears. General anesthesia and sedation are appropriate for patients receiving advanced oral surgical procedures, and those with certain physical and mental handicaps, but should be reserved for only a small minority of highly phobic dental patients. General anesthesia and sedation are considered safe and effective, but cost more and may pose an increased health risk for some patients.

A better option is

> 1) Regression to cause, by an experienced hypnotist, to eliminate the initial sensitizing event (ISE)

> 2) Self-hypnosis training whereby the client can take him/herself into the state of analgesia or anesthesia at will. A script for this is included in the section "Scripts"

What is Dental Anxiety?

While allopathic professionals might call an anxiety a fear, or a phobia, the National Guild of Hypnotists (NGH) refers to the client's presenting issue as an anxiety. The Diagnostic and Statistical Manual of Mental Disorders (DSM-IV) describes dental phobia as a *"marked and persistent fear that is excessive or unreasonable"*.

Does that mean it is a mental disorder? Yes and No. The main problem in defining "dental phobia" is there is no one type of dental phobia, and that there are difference between anxieties, fears and phobias as follows:

1. **Dental Anxiety** is very common, and most people experience it to some degree if they are about to experience, for example, a dental procedure they have never experienced before.

2. **Dental Fear** is a reaction to a known danger, which involves a fight-or-flight response when confronted with the threatening stimulus.

3. **Dental Phobia** is much stronger in that people experience fight-or-flight response just thinking about, or being reminded of the threatening situation. Someone with a dental phobia will avoid dental care at all costs, until either a physical problem or the psychological burden of the phobia becomes overwhelming.

How is Dental Anxiety Measured?

There is a problem with measuring dental phobia and dental anxiety. A patient/client who has "anxiety" of dental work, can find it just as frightening as another person, (who has been diagnosed with a phobia), experiences that phobia.

From the research available, it is hypothesized that dental anxiety proper may be more common in people who are generally anxious. As with any intake interview, the practitioner needs to determine the depth of a client's anxiety from *the client's point of view* on a scale of 1 – 10 so at each session this subjective unit of discomfort can be tested – and in cases of regression to cause can be brought up for hypnoanalysis.

Who most suffers Dental Anxiety?

"Our findings did not suggest any discernible differences [between males and females] in either the reasons given for accessing this online group nor its advantages in terms of coping with the challenges of dental anxiety". *(Buchanan & Coulson, 2007)* Women on the other hand are more likely to talk freely about their dental anxiety while men may feel they must hide it behind their tough exterior.

Studies have noticed that dental phobia appears to be more common in people who suffer from another psychiatric disorder, notably Generalized Anxiety Disorder, agoraphobia, depression, and emetophobia *(intense, irrational fear or anxiety pertaining to vomiting)*. This same research suggests that about 20% of dental phobics also have a concurrent psychiatric disorder.

The Most Common Causes of Dental Anxiety

Bad experiences - dental anxiety leading to a phobia is most often caused by painful dental experiences. This not only includes painful dental visits, but also emotional behaviors such as being humiliated by a dentist.

History of abuse - dental phobia is also common in people who have been sexually abused, particularly in childhood. A history of bullying or having been physically or emotionally abused by a person in authority may also contribute to developing dental phobia, especially in combination with bad experiences with dentists.

Uncaring dentist – dental schools teach that the fear of pain is what will keep people from seeing a dentist, and dental practitioners are intensely trained in chair-side psychology. However, when the dental patient believes the pain is "inflicted" by a dentist who is perceived to be cold and controlling, it has a mental impact. Pain inflicted by a dentist who is perceived as caring however is much less likely to result in psychological trauma *(Weiner et al, 1999)*.

Humiliation – humans are social animals and insensitive remarks by the practitioner or their staff and the intense feelings of humiliation they provoke, are one of the main factors that can cause or contribute to a dental phobia. *(i.e., "don't be such a baby! It's only a needle!")*

Explicit learning - if a parent, caregiver or friend displays anxiety about dental visits the children may "inherit" that response, and even though they may not experience any negative experiences themselves while at the dentist may well be imprinted with that anxiety.

Anxiety around needles – is one learned from the doctor's office as a child (or from a movie) as a fear of being "hurt" with something sharp. Even when they know it is for continuing good health, dramatization and vicarious stories can leave people with an unintended fear they carry into the dental office for self-protection.

PTSD - research indicates people who had negative dental experiences suffer from symptoms very similar to those found in post-traumatic stress disorder (PTSD) patients. This is characterized by intrusive thoughts of the bad experience and nightmares about dentists or dental situations.

Note: Post-Traumatic Dental-care Anxiety (PTDA), may be part of the PTSD spectrum in the forthcoming Diagnostic and Statistical Manual of Mental Disorders, fifth edition (DSM-V), due in May, 2015.

Stefan Bracha and colleagues (2006) in an article in the Hawaii Dental Journal said of dental anxiety: "In this article, we suggest that the term "dental phobia", as commonly applied to the experience of dental fear and anxiety, is typically a misnomer. The problem with using the term "phobia" in a dental-care context is as follows: by definition, phobias involve a fear that is "excessive or unreasonable", which the individual recognizes as such, and in which the anxiety, panic attacks and phobic avoidance are not better accounted for by another disorder, including posttraumatic stress disorder (PTSD). In our experience, most individuals who experience dental anxiety or fear do not view their symptoms as "excessive or unreasonable" and in that sense, resemble individuals with PTSD. Further, our review of the dental-care literature suggests that true (innate) dental phobias (akin to unreasonable fear at the sight of blood or a syringe) probably account for a smaller percentage of cases, and that a larger subset of dental-care anxiety (DA) cases stem from dental experiences that are, at a minimum, aversive and/or painful, and at times highly traumatizing. Research has documented that individuals who reported having experienced painful dental treatments and perceived a lack of control in the dental situation were approximately 14 times more likely to also report higher dental fear, and approximately 16 times more likely to report being less willing to return to the dental treatment. Based on the current available research, we propose that this psychological condition should be conceptualized as Posttraumatic Dental-care Anxiety (PTDA), and should be classified as part of the Posttraumatic Stress Disorder (PTSD) spectrum in the forthcoming Diagnostic and Statistical Manual of Mental Disorders, fifth edition (DSM-V)."

The Impact of Dental Anxiety on Daily Life

Sufferers of dental phobia tend to think that nobody else feels the way they do. Dental anxiety may lead to anxiety and depression. Depending on how obvious is the lack of dental care, the urge to laugh and smile is repressed. People may avoid socializing and meeting people, even close friends, due to embarrassment over their teeth. Regardless of ability, they may also avoid taking on jobs or approaching opportunities involving contact with the public.

Dental phobia sufferers may also avoid doctors for fear that they might want to have a look at their tongue or throat and then suggest that a visit to a dentist might be recommended.

3. OTHER ISSUES TO WORK WITH

HypnoDontics is a natural convincer which springboards the client into improving other areas of their life as easily and comfortably as they did in the dentist's office.

Uses of Hypnosis for Dental Patients

1. Elimination of the patient's tension, anxiety or fear of pain and related discomfort.

2. Accustoming the patient to orthodontic or prosthetic appliances after the patient has agreed to them.

3. Maintenance of the patient's comfort during long and arduous periods of dental work.

4. Modification of unwanted dental habits, such as bruxism, which

is the unconscious grinding of teeth.

5. Reduction of anesthesia *(numbing)* or analgesia *(pain relieving medication)* during dental procedures.

6. Substitution for, or in combination with pre-medication *(i.e., topical)*

7. Prevention of gagging reflex and nausea and the control of salivary flow and bleeding.

8. Increased rapidity of post-procedure healing.

NOTE: Direct suggestion will not be appropriate in all cases. Upon determining treatment direction, once regressed and identifying the Initial Sensitizing Event (ISE) or imprint and having guided the client through forgiveness or parts therapy, the change in belief still takes time to negotiate its way to full conscious awareness and agreement.

There may be any number of other beliefs that arise along the way that need to be additionally addressed, and as with a flying anxiety, for example, you do not want the client negatively rebounding with newly awakened and partially unresolved memories or beliefs half way through the dental appointment.

**That is why the recommendation is to avoid treating dental anxiety issues as a "one appointment fix."

Once the client has happily enjoyed their first ever no-stress dental appointment, they will be very pleased to return and see you for any underlying issues. (See Case History #1)

Useful general suggestions include:

"Now close your mind, and imagine what I tell you is real ... now... notice how you're in the dentist's chair...comfortable.. and see the dentist coming towards you – the closer he gets the calmer you become."

"Salivation is getting less and less. Your mouth is dry and the dentist is able to work on it easily and effortlessly. Salivation just slows down to ten percent and excessive salivation just won't happen. All tension fades away. Tension has been left out in the car, in the car parking lot or area".

"Every time you go to the dentist *you will be more and more comfortable."*

"I have a powerful medicine that can anesthetize this area here (can save money by using some cold water or mint mouthwash). *The depth of this anesthesia it will probably last for "X" hrs. It is so powerful that for some people you'll probably not even be able to feel or even taste it."*

"You're with a professional now, and listening, and sometimes I want you to ask some questions if that's OK. You ask how long is the procedure and if there may be some bleeding involved you give yourself that time and that is the time you tell your body the bleeding stops, and it stops. Instantly it will stop and when I say instantly that means with 15 seconds. If I don't give instructions you will set that anesthesia free and no bleeding, no discomfort of any kind – go through your day naturally without any chemicals at all."

Agoraphobia

Agoraphobia is an anxiety disorder involving fear of public places and open spaces. However, there is an accumulating body of evidence implying that a one-way causal relationship between spontaneous panic attacks and agoraphobia is not prevalent and that agoraphobia actually develops as a complication, not a cause, of panic attacks.

Specifically, it is now thought by the medical community that Agoraphobia may arise by the fear of having a panic attack in a setting from which there is no easy means of escape. Alternatively, social anxiety problems may also be an underlying cause. As a result, sufferers of agoraphobia avoid public and/or unfamiliar places, especially large, open, spaces such as shopping malls or airports where there are few places to hide.

In severe cases, the sufferer may become confined to his or her home, experiencing difficulty traveling from this safe place. This affects approximately 3.2 million adults in the US between the ages of 18 to 54. They certainly avoid the dentist!

Bruxism

Bruxism involves involuntary or unconscious grinding of the teeth, usually during sleep. This grinding can lead to orofacial pain and residual problems with the teeth and gums. Hypnosis has often been found to be effective in controlling bruxism.

American Journal of Clinical Hypnosis in April 1994, reported a 63-year-old woman suffering nocturnal bruxism since the age of three. This habit caused facial pain, ulceration on the inside of one of her cheeks and headaches. During hypnosis she was given suggestions including wakening whenever she felt her jaw tighten or her teeth came together then immediately she would fall back to sleep. Three days later, she reported that she had not ground her teeth at all. Furthermore, the ulceration in her cheek had begun healing and her sleep had improved. At a 60-month follow-up, the patient reported that she was "cured" and her dentist confirmed that damage to her teeth had stopped.

In the author's experience bruxism is almost always about anger: words unsaid going over and over in the mind during the night, and often during the day with the jaw going back and forth "chewing on the regrets". In this case, the most effective treatment is regression to cause with a consulting hypnotist.

Script: Bruxism:

"Stressful situations occur every day, which may cause many people to grit their teeth. Whenever one of these anxiety-producing events happens, or is going to happen, such as …(insert typical problem)*... you unconsciously grit your teeth. Now you have a way of handling the situation, by keeping just enough nervous energy to deal with the task perfectly - and letting go of excess tension. When you're ready to go to sleep at night you can practice, saying 'Nothing is important enough in my life to grind me down.'*

Most teeth grinding happens during the night. The cause is that the subconscious mind remembers the stressful or anxiety producing situations which have occurred during the day, or threaten to occur in the future, and replays them many times during the night. Now during the night, the abnormal touch of your teeth will waken you - you'll smile - realize that your subconscious is protecting you, turn over, and go right back to sleep, losing no sleep at all. It's so nice when you're feeling tired to just rest your head and drift down into a nice, deep, comfortable physiological sleep, and so delightful to be aware of that comfortable feeling that you experience when there is an appropriate amount of space between your teeth - no contact.

And whenever you drift down into a nice, deep, comfortable physiological sleep, there is the possibility that on this night or perhaps on the next night, or that this week or the next week, you will grind your teeth. But from now on, whenever that does occur you will immediately awaken and relax your jaw, before drifting back into that nice, deep, comfortable, physiological sleep. You know, it's a very nice thing to have a good grip of the hand, and people are often so lazy about exercising - they always find a reason not to - but every time you do grind your teeth, you exercise your grip, until you get a really good grip. It's so good to have a nice strong grasp of things. Your unconscious mind knows exactly what I mean and fully grasps everything that it finds gripping. It's also good to let go and relax - and relaxation is something that now comes naturally to you. Letting go of tension is as easy as can be and each time you feel and experience that sense of 'letting go' you deeper into that lovely calm, relaxing feeling."

Gagging - Different Techniques

The gagging reflex interferes with examinations, cleanings, dental x-rays, and treatment as well as holding patients back from their required dental hygiene regime. A fear of gagging and throwing up is a common feature in emetophobia (the fear of vomiting). Emetophobia, coupled with a bad gag reflex, can be terrifying.

Hypnotist Beryl should know – "I used to have it so badly I could not clean my teeth without gagging! A nasal decongestant before my appointment really helped in keeping my nasal passageways open – I knew I could breathe through my nose. I practiced diaphragmatic breathing exercises through my nose to relax in the chair, but it did not go away until I had a few sessions of hypnotherapy. I realized that the first time I gagged was during sexual abuse as a child and in hypnosis, I could release the cry that had to be stifled in me at the time. Now I have been so much better – I can clean my teeth now. At the dentist, while instruments are in my mouth I hum favorite songs in my head. It is impossible to hum and gag at the same time! My dentist knows I used to have the gagging issue and reassures me that he will stop immediately if I tap my thigh twice. I just rinse, or catch my breath.

For many people, there is a sense of loss of control in a dental chair during treatment and the tendency to gag is one representation of this. When there is a trusting relationship, then the sense of control increases. So encourage your client to tell the dentist and establish a signal with them during hypnosis – just knowing it is there and can be used can result in ending the problem.

There are physiological and emotional causes which can predispose or cause a person to gag:

Physiological: causes may include not being able to breathe through your nose properly, catarrh, sinusitis, nasal polyps, a dry mouth, mucus in the upper respiratory tract, and medications that cause nausea as a side effect. Medical conditions such as gastrointestinal diseases, anxiety disorders, can also contribute to gagging. Gagging can be worse in the morning for some people, suggest scheduling appointments in the afternoon.

Emotional causes: Sitting up rather than lying down can also help with the gag reflex. "In some situations, unconventional measures may be required. Dentists have had to take impressions with the patient standing up to help stop the gag reflex. Some people gag because they have been abused in the past (see our case studies). We have found a high percentage of clients who have been sexually abused. Sometimes it is about desensitizing to smells.

4. WORKING WITH THE DENTIST

Q. How do you convince the dentist that hypnosis is tremendously helpful to their patients?

   A. Offer the dental practitioner a free session!

Dentists are people like anyone else and industry-specific studies reveal they are often under more stress than physicians. So learn about and understand how chair-side anxiety and stress affects the dentist

In a September, 2008 article published in Oral Health and Dental Practice Management, *Canada's leading dental journal, Dr. Randy Lang. DDS, D.Ortho., wrote about stress in dentistry. He found that* dental literature confirmed that dentists are subject to a variety of stress-related physical and emotional problems. These problems occurred at an alarmingly high incidence that surpassed even that of physicians, involving cardiovascular disease, ulcers, colitis, hypertension, lower back pain, eye strain, marital disharmony, alcoholism, drug addiction, mental depression and suicide.

As reported by Dr. Lang, personality traits that characterize a good dentist are also traits that predispose to depression in mid-life, drug and alcohol abuse and the attendant risk of suicide.

Among such traits are:
1. Compulsive attention to details;
2. Extreme conscientiousness;
3. Careful control of emotions;
4. Unrealistic expectations of themselves and others (i.e. employees and patients); and,
5. A marked dependence on individual performance and prestige.

Patient Anxiety Stressors

International studies reveal that nervous patients are among the top 5 practice stressors for the dentist, and the psychological stress of working with apprehensive and fearful patients can be worrying to the dental practitioner.

Dentists may experience patterns of physiological stress responses *(increased heart rate, high blood pressure, sweating, etc.)* which parallel the patient's responses when performing dental procedures which evoke patient fear and anxiety. This in turn can lead to an early heart attack for the dentist.

Compromised Treatment Frustration

Another of the top 5 associated stressors for the dentist is compromised treatment frustration. In Canada, a dentist spends four years in dental school learning the "ideal" treatment for their future patients. Yet the realities of private practice are that many patients, due to financial restraints, poor insurance plans or low appreciation of quality dental care, will not accept "ideal" treatment plans.

Consequently, the dentist is often forced to operate a "fix-and-repair" business, providing compromised treatment for patients who refuse the full spectrum of dental care. The dentist then ends up emotionally carrying the responsibility for less than ideal results while the patient continues to express unrealistic expectations.

Dental Practice Stress Synopsis

In Denmark, a study probing dentists' perceived stress and its relation to perception about anxious patients echoed similar studies conducted globally, and found dentist perceptions of their most intense stressors were ranked as:

1. Running behind schedule *(Murphy's Law+)*
2. Causing pain**
3. Heavy workload
4. Late patients
5. Anxious patients**

On the other hand, perceived causes of dental anxiety by patients by importance were ranked as:

- Fear of pain**
- Trauma in dental treatment**
- General psychological problems
- Shame about dental status
- Economic excuses *(ability to pay)*

Script to Help a Dentist (C)

This script is useful to give as a complimentary session with your local dentist, maybe with the Hartland ego-strengthening script used as a deeper following induction.

Induction of Choice … Deepen… followed by:

Life is good and the present moment commands your focused attention. You are relaxed and interested as you begin the intake interview. You ask about previous experiences with hypnosis and search out your patient's attitudes, beliefs and questions about their required dental work.

From deep within your own center, your confident voice calmly resonates. Your eyes radiate strength, courage, and compassion. Your appearance, your voice, and your methods of communication all express confidence in yourself, in your skills, and in your ability to help others.

Your manner is relaxed and assured. You easily express the right word, the right phrase, the right gesture, and the appropriate feeling when communicating with your client…. you readily enter into the world of your patient.

You listen openly and with focused attention to what your patient has to say. And, because you are competent, skilled and knowledgeable, you speak easily and with authority. Your patients are eager to have the work done by you. They appreciate your poise, your experience, your skill and your caring. Your patients' expectations make you feel more and more confident. You feel good.

Your patients are relaxed and trusting you, for they sense your deep interest in them. You are positive, persuasive and a force for good. Your highest desire is to bring joy and happiness into the lives of others. You now realize that you are a talented and highly creative person. You use what you have chosen from all that you have learned, wisely, safely, appropriately and sincerely.

Each time you work with a patient you feel an exhilarating surge of confidence and enthusiasm. You easily remember your many successful and rewarding experiences in helping other patients and everything you've read, studied and heard in courses easily comes to you. You are highly skilled at understanding and guiding others, and you easily accept the praise and approval that others give to you.

Your work and new confidence brings to you emotional, intellectual, social and financial eminence among your peers, and you are rapidly moving towards the satisfaction of your deepest needs and the realization of your highest goals.

And so it is…. Now each of these suggestions continues making a permanent, deep, vivid impression on your subconscious mind. Each day in your daily life, you will become more and more aware of the full, powerful, positive creative expression of these ideas.

From this time forward, with each passing day, you become more and more aware of a personal feeling of well-being and confidence-Confidence that each day brings you one step closer to each of your goals. You plan and arrange your daily schedule with care.

You allow yourself time for personal recreation and relaxation. It is easy for you to keep to your schedule because you plan it so well.

From deep within your own center, your confidence calmly resonates. Your eyes radiate strength, courage, and compassion. Your appearance, your voice, and your methods of communication all express confidence in yourself, in your skills and in your ability to help others. Your hands are relaxed, steady and true. Your manner is relaxed and assured.

You easily express the right word, the right phrase, the right gesture, and the appropriate feeling when communicating with your patient. Your patients are relaxed and trusting of you for they sense your deep interest in them. You are positive, persuasive and a force for good. Your highest desire is to bring joy and happiness into the lives of others. You stimulate wonderful, positive and exciting thoughts and feelings in the people you counsel. Your hands are relaxed, steady and true. Your manner is relaxed and assured.

You now realize that you are an exceptionally talented and highly creative person. You use what you have chosen from all that you have learned.

Each of these suggestions continues making a permanent, deep, vivid impression on your subconscious mind. Each day in your daily life, you will become more and more aware of the full, powerful, positive creative expression of these ideas …. and so it is … EMERGE

5. HOW TO EXPAND INTO THE WORLD OF HYPNODONTICS

How to approach the dental practitioner

1. Rather than calling for an appointment, approach their office as you would to make any "sales" call and dress as you would for a job interview.

2. Ensure you have 10 or so brochures to leave for the practitioner's patients, as well as a covering, or introductory letter, for the dentist.

3. Instead of a generalized cover-all letter, address your letter directly to the dental practitioner(s), and sign each personally with a blue pen.

4. The introductory letter should be maximum 4 paragraphs on one page. A single bio-page can be included as a stand-alone second page.

5. Be prepared to speak to and impress the office manager/ appointment secretary rather than the dentist on your first visit. ***They are your gateway into the dentist.***

6. The brochure is your professional statement and should be in full color rather than black and white, and printed on glossy paper rather than plain, printer paper. Rather than leaving a hundred or so, only leave 10 brochures with the dental office until you speak personally to the dentist, or receive permission to leave more for display in the dentist's reception area.

7. Write and ***rehearse, rehearse***, and ***rehearse again*** your 30-second elevator speech. This may be all the time you get at the front desk, and first impressions are your stock in trade.

8. Remember that the dental surgeon is the medical expert and we offer a complimentary therapy to assist the professional in their work. So leave the big words at home – most dentists have forgotten more tongue-twisting multi-syllabic words than you have ever learned.

HOW TO COMPOSE A GREAT 30-SECOND ELEVATOR SPEECH

Your 30-second "elevator" speech can be the difference between working or not working! So, here we learn how to construct one.

First, it is not about you. In as short a statement as possible, draw a situation from real life that we all experience *(nerves before a speech/test/exam, dental/medical anxiety, weight loss/self-confidence, etc.)* and then tell people *what measurable results you deliver,* and *who you deliver them to.* Then shut up.

Do not tell them EVERYTHING in one breath. Tell them something that is so powerfully grabbing that they just have to ask you for more, and even then when you respond - keep it short - keep them asking for more.

How Do You Do That? Try this exercise that can change not only how you present yourself, but often it goes so deep that it will even change your vision of who and what you are …

Take out a sheet of paper and create 3 columns. Consider this activity as a work in progress that will continually change not just as you work your way through it, but it should get you thinking so that you will continually come back to the worksheet to make the answers better and better throughout your career.

At first, do not worry about getting "the perfect" speech as much as just getting something down on paper to start the thinking process. You can re-visit it as many times as you want to make it better and better.

Remember, this is not about you … it is about helping your potential clients meet their goals in life. Avoid going on and on about your training, or telling client stories ad nauseam. Be realistic. If you sound too good to be true, you will just sound like another person flogging another "can't lose deal."

1st Column - Far Left: Services

List your products, services and/or features down this column. For most people this has been what you have been telling the world that you do or sell. List each and every social and physical issue you work with.

2nd Column - To The Right: Benefits

For every item in the column to the left, directly across from each one write what is the benefit of that service or technique. After you have written down why someone should invest in your services, ask yourself why someone would even want whatever it was you wrote down there. Keep asking yourself why, why, why until you have gotten down to the real bottom-line of why someone should use your services.

3rd Column – Measurable Results

- This is the most powerful statement for your marketing. Consider the measurements and how you will present them. You can state a fact that a client typically gets ___, or, you guarantee a minimum result of _____, etc.

- Tell people that *AT A MINIMUM, I GUARANTEE* they will walk out of my office feeling measurably better than they did when they came in, naturally, without drugs, PLUS show them how to do it for themselves.

- Making your results immediately measurable gives them a very visual perceived value for what you do for your clients. People buy your services based on the value they perceive you will deliver, so vividly show them that value, and make it so visual that they do not have to guess.

It helps to go back to "Why buy the service?" and revise it. Once you start to revise the benefits of self-hypnosis, you will come up with more measurable results. So feel free to review, change, and go through it again. And... get out there and use it! Over the next few weeks keep looking for the ideal measurement, and come back to revise it again and again. It will keep getting better.

One of Rev. Timothy Jones' elevator speeches is:

"It's estimated that 80% of all North Americans avoid going to their dentist due to anxiety. By using self-hypnosis, you can quickly, comfortably and easily drift off to your favorite holiday spot for an hour every time you relax in the dentist's chair. You can probably hear the relaxing sound of that beach in the back of your mind right now, can't you? So rather than avoiding the dentist, we show you how to easily summon up a holiday and bring it to life so you don't even notice what the dentist is doing. Does that sound like something you'd prefer to do"

Play with what you say at social events. Say it one way and watch the results. Practice, practice, practice! Say it in front of a mirror, repeat it emphasizing different words while driving, or tease your friends with it.

Measure the results of your elevator speech by

- The noise level of the room after you say it

- How many people approach you during the event

- How many approach you when they see you in the future.

Change the words just a little each time you deliver it, and keep track of the ones that work the best, and watch your business, and referrals, grow quickly.

The ease by which you verbalize the imagery of your 30-second elevator speech will also change your vision about who you are and who you can become!

How to Advertise

Web Page - A web page is the most efficient way to advertise at minimal cost. It is constant, available to all at any time and can explain your procedure, the myths and truths of hypnosis, your method of treatment, billing procedure and availability. Its advantage over a brochure is that you can edit it anytime, and it is open 24/7.

Brochures - Full color brochures run about a dollar each, and you should have the editable design on your computer so you can change your information at any time. We have found printing runs of a thousand at a time a waste of money because when you want to make changes, you are left with useless copies. We suggest you only print 50-100 at a time, and they be printed off your thumb drive by a copy shop using a professional level color printer.

Community Newspapers - Your local paper is a great place to place an inexpensive ad, and inquiries should be directed to your web page, rather than to your own telephone.

Professional Magazines - Advertising in professional magazines works sometimes. The dental profession is very connected, so word of mouth is always the most effective advertiser.

Dental Offices - When approaching dental offices, you will generally find 3 types of dentists.

1. This type does not think they need any help at all and although they will be polite, they do not want to hear from you.

2. The second type is experienced enough to be interested in alternatives for their patients, and will keep you in mind.

3. The third type has had memorable experiences with patient anxiety and will be only too glad, to have their patients' concerns addressed by a specialist.

You will also find 3 types of office managers, or receptionists.

1. One type is painfully polite and will take your material to give to the dentist.

2. The second type can be quite arrogant - THEY themselves are the dentist and need no help!

3. This type greets you enthusiastically and shows great personal interest in HypnoDontics.

Q. How often will you actually speak to the dental practitioner directly when cold calling practices?

> **A.** Not often. Their days are packed and their lunch hour, if they even take one, belongs to them, or emergencies - not you - which is why we leave written material for them to consider.

Advertising to the Public

If you wait for a dentist to call you, you are going to wait a long time. It is not that they do not want their patients to see someone else, but with a dentist almost in every corner plaza nowadays, they now offer sleep (pill/gas) treatment just to encourage patients to come to and stay with them.

The most graphic example of the great strength of HypnoDontics is an anxious patient who seeks out the hypnotist on their own then goes back to their dentist as calm as a cucumber.

One client was a nurse who could only tolerate half of a root canal procedure before calling it off. She came to me with a temporary cap dreading going back for completion of the repair. Two sessions and three days later she went back for her appointment and the dentist was so amazed at the difference she exclaimed, *"Good grief Sharon! What HAPPENED? I can hardly believe the difference!"*

Keep in mind that the dentist charges for the procedure, not by the hour, so they have a vested interest in completing the work expeditiously. Literally, they cannot afford to dilly dally around with anxious patients.

Word Of Mouth and Referrals

After a while, you will not need advertising. Once you get 2 or 3 professionals realizing good results from your work, the word spreads quickly in your area. in the same way, dental patients will rave about you to their friends.

What to Say to the Dentist

In your own words, explain what the dental professional already knows, but may not recently have considered while setting up their practice ... as listed below.

The alleviation of fear and anxiety is of as much aid to the client as any anesthetic procedure. Excessive salivation and bleeding can be controlled hypnotically, the gagging reflex can be subdued, the client's ability to tolerate dental appliances can be increased, and healing can be more easily facilitated following any procedure.

Experienced dentists, oral surgeons, or orthodontists will readily considering referring their patients to a Consulting Hypnotist if they believe it will benefit their patients.

NOTE: Do not forget to offer the dental practitioner an industry-specific "stress-buster" session as a professional courtesy at no obligation, and inform them that training them and/or their staff in the basics of guided imagery for relaxation can be turned into CEU's by their professional association.

STRUCTURING THE CLIENT APPOINTMENT

The most commonly asked client question after *"how much is it?"* is *"how many sessions does it take?"*

As much as the authors and our collaborators do not believe in "one-session" fixes, at the least, HypnoDontics can readily ameliorate the tension, nervousness and unreasonable fear of pain, often exhibited by anxious dental clients within one appointment. Depending on how close the dental appointment is to the HypnoDontics session. **This does not include hypno-numbing.

In an ideal world, the Consulting Hypnotist would meet with the anxious dental patient a good week before the scheduled dental appointment, then follow up with a second reinforcing appointment the day before, or if possible, the day of the dental appointment.

The first appointment is to introduce the client to hypnosis and establish their "safe place" or comfort zone where they will go during the dental appointment (ninety percent of the author's clients prefer a beach).

While in a somnambulistic state, embed a post-hypnotic suggestion that they will easily be able to relax deeply and enjoy drifting off to (their safe place) as soon as they sit down in the dental chair, or enter the dental office. Assign a physical anchor to lock in the state, like the joining together of the thumb and first finger. The first session can also be a great place to give a post-hypnotic suggestion for an instant induction in subsequent sessions with you.

The Most Asked Question

Consulting Hypnotists most often ask if hand-to-face numbing is appropriate during the first visit. Depending on the natural abilities of the client, most are quite able to enter a somnambulistic state and numb their fingers and transfer that numbness to a facial area during the first visit.

However, how well they can reproduce that effect in a dental setting the next day, or the day after that, takes practice, which is why the author suggests a second appointment.

The initially embedded anchors for relaxation on the first visit work quite well any time up to a week or so later, which, when invoked, increases client belief in the process, consequently increasing the credibility of the

Consulting Hypnotist. However, the vast majority of our clients require a 2nd visit when they allow themselves to go into a deeper state which provides for a deeper, longer lasting experience.

Consulting Hypnotists should be reminded that the ability lies within the client, not in the script, and the hypnotherapeutic objectives of single appointments, although they may provide immediate relief, need to be reinforced for lasting change.

"Working in the somnambulistic state is key".

Backup CD's for the Client?

There have always been two sides to the question as to whether hypnotherapeutic practitioners should make CD's for their clients.

One school of thought believe a take-home CD can help reinforce conditioning for the client, while the other group believe if they mass produce CD's, then why would clients bother to see a Consulting Hypnotist at all?

Most of us fall somewhere in the middle.

It can be argued that it is counterproductive to make Smoking, Weight Loss, etc., CDs to distribute in your own marketplace because in an instant gratification society, people might be more likely to buy the CDs rather than spend the actual time with a trained hypnotist whose fees may range anywhere from $90 to $150+ per hour.

However, for the dental client specifically, once they have invested the time with a practitioner, it only makes sense to continue their anxiety "conditioning" in the time leading up to their appointment in the form of a maintenance CD *(MP3/4)*.

With a take-home CD, the client can continue reinforcing their new beliefs on their own time, as well as in the dental chair intra-procedure.

When approached, quite often the dentist will ask for a copy of the reinforcing CD the Consulting Hypnotist intends to provide to their patients and will listen to it **1**) out of curiosity and **2**) to use as part of their decision-making process depending on how professional it sounds.

LETTER TO THE RECEIVING DENTAL SURGEON

Once we have hypnotherapeutically prepared an anxious dental client, we give them a letter to take to their dentist. The letter lets the dentist know how to work with their patient in a pre-conditioned entrained state, how to emerge them, and what words to use to promote a calm state of mind and promote healing.

Once a dentist work with a hypnotherapeutically prepared patient vs. the anxious patient, s/he immediately notices the difference chair-side. Dr. Nora Powell of Dubai London Clinic often says to me *"I had one of yours in the other day, Beryl"* with a smile on her face. She is one of many dentists who refer clients for HypnoDontics.

In our experience, there will always be a group of dentists, who believe they have all the skills and training required to calm a patient. In fact, one dental practitioner said if he could not work with someone, that he just "gassed them", meaning inhalation anesthesia. That attitude however is fast fading.

Mostly, the dental profession has always been hypnosis-friendly and many dentists are open to hypnosis to help their patients. As long as the HypnoDontics Practitioner exhibits the level of professionalism they expect of their own staff and fellow professionals, they will gladly work with a Consulting Hypnotist.

In fact, once the dentist agrees to display the Consulting Hypnotist's brochures in the reception area, the number of patients who ask for more details will surprise them.

Once we have hypnotherapeutically prepared an anxious dental client, we give them a letter (following) to take to their dentist.

Although a couple of pages long, the following letter lets the dentist know how to deepen and work with their patient in a trance state, how to emerge them, and what words to use to promote a calm state of mind and promote healing.

A concerned dental practitioner will read the letter and integrate the procedure into their own particular chair-side style. Please feel free to adjust to your own situation.

Your Letterhead

Current Date

ATTN: Dr. Great Dentist

RE: Your Patient, Ms. I.M. Anxious

Your patient I.M. Anxious has been hypnotherapeutically prepared for dental surgery.

Specifically, we have addressed anxiety issues surrounding her procedure. Please note that we have NOT conditioned your patient to self-induce anesthesia, but that her conditioning is to neurolinguistically reframe the sensations arising from a dental procedure to minimize anxiety.

BEFORE the PROCEDURE

Upon application of the initial topical anesthetic, we have given your patient post-hypnotic suggestions implying that although their physical body is in your office, their mind will drift to a pre-visualized "safe place" where they will feel only slight pressure in the area where you are working.

May we suggest that you consider using similar terminology before the injection. You can suggest to them that they may feel "only a slight pressure" in that area of the jaw for a few seconds as you prepare the area, rather than using the words needle or injection, as they have not been de-sensitized to those words as much as the sensation arising out of the action. It has been reframed to feeling only "a slight pressure" in the area where you are working.

DURING the PROCEDURE

Similarly, some key phrases employed during the HypnoDontics session were, "feeling calm and relaxed."

When using a mechanized tool and other instruments, the movement and sounds tends to draw them away from their visualization slightly. You can minimize their anxiety if you repeat our embedded suggestions ... *"although you will always hear the sound of my voice, any noises you hear around you of my equipment will fade into the background and only serve to relax you further ..."*

We avoid the use of words that have negative connotations for your patient, like "drill," instead replacing it by telling them you are going to "buff, clean or irrigate" the area and that "you may feel some vibration which will comfort you even more."

While involved in the dental procedure, your patient can readily respond to your instructions to her regarding head movement and jaw positioning. You may also find that your patient may require a rubber/silicone "donut" device to help keep her jaw extended, as in her relaxed state, she may inadvertently start to close her mouth.

Although your patient can hear you and your dental assistant talking during the whole procedure, if you address her directly, i.e., asking her questions (vs. giving her directions), the effort to answer you could tend to bring her up a level or two from her pre-conditioned entrainment.

Additionally, we suggest to surgeons that they consider reframing any conversation between their staff present to be on a positive note. For example, to exclaim, *"My lord, this is a deep one. I don't know if I can get it all"* may leave residual effects on healing. Instead, numerous peer-reviewed studies have proven that positive post-operative healing is more rapidly realized when the surgeon emphasizes intra-procedure how well things are going, how quickly the area is going to heal, etc.

Even though substantive research has not answered the question as to why it specifically occurs, if you suggest to your patient (by name), while in trance, that she or he "turn off" or "turn down" the level of bleeding or salivation in the area of the procedure, her body will respond appropriately. Similarly, suggestion that she "increase" the level of bleeding or salivation will also elicit her body will respond appropriately.

When you do invoke this physiologic phenomenon, remember to "turn it back on", or "off" as the case may be, "to normal response levels" at the appropriate time in your procedure.

FOLLOWING the PROCEDURE

Your patient is experienced in bringing herself to full awareness in the room, on a five-count, when you tell her the procedure is finished. We suggest the dental practitioner consider ensuring their patient is indeed fully aware before leaving by counting them up from five to one (or one to five), with suggestions that pre-suppose healthy healing and reduction of post-operative swelling or discomfort.

An example might be –

"Now, I'm going to count up from one to five, and then I'll say, "Fully aware." When I say the number five, your eyes will open and you will be fully aware, feeling calm, rested, refreshed, and relaxed.

All right. One - slowly, calmly, easily, you are returning to your full awareness once again, secure in the knowledge that the procedure went very well, and that you will heal quickly and comfortably.

Two - each muscle and nerve in your body is loose and limp and relaxed, and you feel wonderfully good in every way.

Three - from head to toe, you are feeling perfect in every way. Physically perfect, mentally perfect, emotionally calm and serene.

Four - your eyes begin to feel sparkling clear under your eyelids, and on the next number I count, your eyelids will open, you'll be fully aware, feeling calm, rested, refreshed, relaxed, invigorated, full of energy, and perhaps even slightly hungry (*a patient cannot feel nauseous and hungry at the same time.*)

Number Five, number five *(with authority)* ... open your eyes, open your eyes (practitioner should gently snap their fingers at this point as an audible, external anchor to the patient) – you are fully aware now. Eyes open. Fully aware!. Fully aware!. Take a good, deep breath, fill up your lungs and stretch, feeling absolutely wonderful in every way."

NOTE that your patient is still slightly in-state for the first two or three minutes after opening their eyes following a session, and are still accepting of positive suggestions (and equally susceptible to negative ones).

NOTE: Your patient should be able to respond to normal conversation at this point. If you detect any confusion or hesitation in their responses, they could still be enjoying an entrained state, in which case you can ask them to close their eyes again and give them a 1 - 3 count, with your voice becoming more authoritative as you reach the number three.

Many practitioners take advantage of this entrainment window to re-emphasize how well the procedure went, how rapidly they will heal with a minimum of discomfort, etc.

If you have any questions or queries, or if you would like to discuss HypnoDontics for another of your patients, please feel free to call anytime.

Perhaps I might suggest too that many dental practitioners also take advantage of hypnotherapy sessions to personally relieve their own anxiety after working with nervous or fearful patients, which can take its own toll on your practice.

Please feel free to call any time. I look forward to hearing from you.

Sincerely Yours,

XXXXX

Board Certified Consulting Hypnotherapist

6. STRUCTURING THE CLIENT APPOINTMENT

1. THE PRE-TALK

The Pre-talk is most important for gaining rapport and trust in you the hypnotists, and your opportunity to train your client about hypnosis. Two key elements can stop hypnosis from taking place:

- fear of hypnosis
- distrust of the hypnotist

We must clear these before hypnosis takes place

When dealing with anxious clients it is very important to explain what hypnosis is and is not and to explain the different roles of the three minds: unconscious, subconscious and conscious.

It is helpful to have your pre-talk on video which can be sent via email to your client before they arrive. Alternatively ask them to arrive early and watch your recorded pre-talk in your waiting room. The mental expectancy after seeing you on screen is "S/he is good, knows their stuff, this is going to help me".

Misinformation to be cleared up before the actual hypnosis includes these seven areas:

1. **Some people mistakenly think that hypnosis is not safe**. That is false. Hypnosis is a normal state of consciousness. Unfortunately, few people make good use of it on their own. You go in and out of hypnotic states several times each day. Some common places you experience natural hypnosis are while riding in or driving an automobile, while watching TV or a movie, and while daydreaming.

2. **Some people mistakenly think that a hypnotist can control them**. That is false. The client is always in control and always decides whether to cooperate with suggestions.

3. **Some people mistakenly think that they might reveal some deep, dark secret while in hypnosis**. That is false. You are more alert in hypnosis, so if you would not tell the hypnotist something now, you certainly would not when in hypnosis. You would just say, "That is none of your business." Yes, you can talk and communicate while in hypnosis. You can even laugh if something strikes you as funny.

4. **Some people mistakenly think that they might not "wake up."** That is false. Hypnosis is not sleep, so there is nothing from which to "wake up" You are four- or five- times more aware than in your normal state of mind. If need be, you would immediately remove the relaxation from your body and return to normal awareness.

5. **Some people mistakenly think that they cannot be hypnotized.** That is false. Everyone capable of understanding is capable of being hypnotized. However, hypnosis is a 100% cooperative effort, so you can always choose not to go into hypnosis. It is always your choice to go into hypnosis. It is always your choice to go deeper into hypnosis. It is always your choice to stay in hypnosis. While in hypnosis, it is always your choice to whether to follow the suggestions you hear.

6. **Some people mistakenly think that they lose consciousness when hypnotized.** That is false. Consciousness is heightened during hypnosis. You will be even more aware of what is going on. Your hearing will improve while in hypnosis. Your thinking will be clearer. Your body may appear to be asleep, but your mind will be much more alert than normal. Imagination, concentration and memory all dramatically improve while in hypnosis.

7. **Some people mistakenly think that a hypnotist can make them do bad things that they would not normally do.** That is false. Any suggestion that violates any strongly held feeling, moral, ethical or religious belief will be automatically rejected by both your conscious mind and your unconscious mind.

Where do such *silly ideas* come from? I do not know for sure, but I think a lot comes from Hollywood script writers who jazz up their stories. In addition, some of it may come from misunderstanding what is happening during a stage show.

Clients should know that:

- Hypnosis is safe

- Hypnosis is fun

- Hypnosis can change your life

2. SUGGESTIBILITY AND CONVINCERS

The client/patient needs to know that they can go into hypnosis easily. For this, we use Suggestibility tests as convincers. Following the hypnosis session they want to know hypnosis took place, so we use convincers. They will not go ahead with dental procedures unless sure hypnosis took place and "something happened".

Vise Suggestibility Test

Grasp client's hands by wrists. Hold them out in front with palms together.

Put your hands together like this... Make a double fist …. Do you know what a vise is?

Close down your eyes and pretend your hands are in a vise. Squeeze them together and pretend they are in a vise. The vise is holding them together. Your hands are in the vise and it is squeezing them tighter and tighter and tighter... Pretend they are in a vise...

Now I'm going to count from one to three... and on the count of three you are going to TRY to pull them apart... but you are not going to be able to do so as your hands are in a vise.

So number one the hands are tight strongly held together...

Two... They are held together just like they are stuck together with glue...

Three... take them apart, you cannot, open them up, you cannot, Number THREE... take them apart... you cannot...

Now just let them relax and they'll come right apart.. …

relax and they come right apart...

(speak faster and keep repeating) …. Keep going until they are apart...

Slowly means creativity & good subject. *No movement means analytical.*

Eye Catalepsy

(Optionally, place your right thumb on the bridge of the subject's nose and apply slight pressure)

I'm going to count from five down to one. As I do, your eyelids lock so tightly closed that the more you try to open them, the tighter they are locking closed.

Five, your eyes are pressing down tightly.

Four, pressing down and sealing shut.

Three, sealing as if they were glued.

Two, they are locked shut. The more you try to open them, the tighter they are locking closed.

Okay, try to open your eyelids now and find them locking tighter and tighter. That's fine. You can stop trying now. Just relaxed and go deeper.

Arm up Convincer

We are going to change all the energy in your body now.

You desire now to operate with only positive force… positive energy...

You would like to be positive all the time now wouldn't you?

We are going to remove from your body any negative energy...

Remove all the negative energy from the body

We are going to do that using your right arm...

We are going to take the arm by the wrist

We are going to put the arm up in the air just like that… Strong and solid

It stays up all by itself...

In fact if I try to push the arm down it comes back up again

Any downward movement and the arm comes right back up again

In fact the arm is so strong that even if you TRY to lower that arm

you will be unable to do so...

So I am going to count to three...

On the count of three you are going to try but you will not be able to do so because any downward movement in that arm and it will pop right back up again...

So One... the arm is stiff and rigid just like a bar of steel.

Number two... The arm is so strong and powerful.

Number three... you try to lower it but you cannot...

You try... you cannot.. try harder... you cannot... try harder it doesn't lower

Because as hard as you try you cannot lower that arm...

because your life now is changing... your energy is changing... your body is changing...

Now you are going to be able to get everything you want

Now stop trying to lower the arm as the energy within your body changes

Now stop trying to lower the arm as the energy within your body totally changes...

When you feel a burst of energy come into your body nod your head

When you feel a burst of energy come into your body nod your head

3. INDUCTION

We recommend using rapid and instant inductions and have found that 99% clients will reach somnambulism with Elman's inductions. The scripts for these are in the section for dentists.

4. DEEPENING

It is very important to deepen to anesthesia level if working alongside the dentist, and test for that. For working with dental surgery you may want to ensure the client is in the coma state however most work will be done in somnambulism.

5. THE WORK: Choose: Direct Suggestion – Parts Therapy or Regression to Cause

A. DIRECT SUGGESTION

This is the basic technique of hypnosis, the compounding of new and positive thought processes which are believed will help the client. Unfortunately, it takes much compounding and many trips to the hypnotist, even playing CD's at home. Scripts can be downloaded online and it is the easiest form of hypnosis, some would argue merely guided imagery. Many of the scripts included in this book are direct suggestion and not recommended as a one-off cure.

B. PARTS THERAPY

Dave Elman and Charles Tebbets used this Client Centered approach, and this NLP 6-Step Reframe is an excellent technique to use whenever there is an inner conflict detected, i.e. a part of me wants this change, a part of me doesn't. A useful source is Roy Hunter's book "Hypnosis for Inner Conflict Resolution"

1. **Set up "yes/no" signals with the subconscious.** Induce hypnosis to somnambulism and set up ideo-motor responses, i.e. use the index fingers of the right and left hand for a yes and no respectively.

2. **Identify a pattern of behavior to be changed.** "I thank the brain for everything you do for (client). We are not our behavior. We are our good intention. We have changed many things in the past, for example (client) you used to wear diapers, do you wear them now (wait for yes or no finger). You know the behavior you would like to change. Now, talk to the subconscious part of you that is causing this behavior and thank it for serving you in whatever way it has. Let it know that you realize it has a positive intention in displaying this behavior."

3. **Break State. Confirm yes/no signals with the subconscious. Request willingness for conscious to know the reason behind the behavior.**

   a. Ask the subconscious mind to confirm yes/no signals by raising the index fingers. (i.e. right index finger raised for 'yes', left index finger raised for 'no'.) Thank the subconscious once the signals have been established.

   b. Ask, "Are you willing to allow the conscious mind to know what it is of value when it _____ *(behavior)*?" If 'yes', say "Good. You can go ahead and let the conscious know what the value is behind _____ (the behavior), and when you've done that, give me a 'yes' signal." If 'no', proceed.

4. **Creating and evaluating new alternatives.**

   a. "Ask the subconscious if it would be willing to go into your creative resources and find 3 new ways of achieving this positive value other than _____ *(behavior)*. (The subconscious is under no obligation to accept or use these choices, but only to find them.)"

   b. "When you get a 'yes', thank the subconscious again. Tell it to go ahead, and give you a 'yes' signal when it has the 3 new alternatives.

   c. "Ask the subconscious to evaluate each choice in terms of whether it believes the choice is at least as immediate, effective and available as ___ *(behavior)*. Each time the subconscious identifies one alternative that it believes is a viable alternative, have it give you a 'yes' signal.

    d.   If you get less than three 'yes', go back to the beginning of Step 4 until you have three new alternatives.

5. Select one alternative.

    a.   "Ask the subconscious to select the new alternative it considers the most satisfying and available in achieving the positive value of____ *(behavior)* that you identified earlier, and to give you a 'yes' signal when it has selected the best alternative".

    b.   "Ask the subconscious if it would be willing to try this new alternative in appropriate situations in the future". Wait for a 'yes' signal, before proceeding.

6. Future-Pace. "Ask the subconscious to imagine future situations of trying out this new behavior in the appropriate context, like trying on a new pair of shoes. Walk around in appropriate situations to see how this new behavior feels. How does it affect others around you? Are there any harmful side effects?

Ask all parts of the subconscious if there are any objections to using this new behavior. Make sure all parts agree." I often ask them to scan their bodies and mind to make sure. Have them notify you with either a 'yes' if it is working, or a 'no' if it is not. If the answer is 'yes', you have a new behavior. If not, go back to the beginning of Step 4 and generate some new alternatives.

C. REGRESSION TO CAUSE

There are several ways to regress to the cause of anxiety or gagging/TMJ, the purpose being to review what happened, what was said, who were "the players", and to feel "the movie" in a new, more adult way, forgive the players, go through subsequent sensitizing events and deal with anything unpleasant that may be remaining. There are hypnotists that evade using regression however it is the authors' preferred technique, effective and in our experience once used effectively with a client the anxiety does not return.

How to use the Affect-Bridge (Regression to Cause)

1.   Induce hypnosis. (Check - must have somnambulism.)

2.   Have the client imagine an incident that would cause the anxiety/ fear they have been feeling. (Make client feel the anxiety/fear and then count 1-10 with each number increasing the feeling.)

3.   Say, "Now this feeling has a beginning, it knows where it came from - follow this fear back to the first time you felt that fear." (Ask

questions such as...day or night? inside or outside? look around what's happening?)

4. Fade scene, analyze and change perception. Then to next conscious event, analyze and change perception, until you have covered all conscious events and have changed subject's perception of each event. Forgiving people then forgiving self may be also necessary here.

5. Then say, *"The more you would become afraid, the calmer you become. What has happened in the past has no effect on you. Now those fears are nothing more than historical events that no longer have any ability to cause you fear now."*

6. Recreate all conscious events to show the real cause of the fear and show that, that fear no longer has any ability to cause the client fear now. Try to feel the fear now.

7. Say, *"You are incapable of feeling any fear of these events."*

8. Say, *"And now I want you to create that situation you find most frightening and try to feel the fear, and the more you try to create the fear, the less it will happen."*

9. **Do grey room technique (if time – or leave for second session)**

10. **Second session if necessary: -** *Have client re-live previous fearful events to determine effectiveness. Reinforce good feelings, with ego strengthening.*

For excellent step by step regression techniques see "Hypnosis and Hypnotherapy" by Banyan and Kein as well as the excellent DVD series produced by www.omnihypnosis.com.

6. EMERGING

We recommend using the word *"emerging"* from hypnosis as the use of "awake" continues the belief that hypnosis is sleep.

While counting the client out of hypnosis, is a good time to reinforce all the work and suggestions made while in the state of trance.

If you use counting down to induce hypnosis, it is preferable to use counting up to emerge, and with positive suggestions.

Section 3

TO THE DENTIST & DENTAL PRACTITIONER

This section for dentists is divided into six sections:

1. What hypnosis can do for you - The Dentist
2. Dentists and stress
3. What a consulting hypnotist can do for your patients
4. What the dentist can do with simple hypnotic techniques
5. Six Steps to hypnosis for dental work
6. Hypnosis in Dental Schools

1. WHAT HYPNOSIS CAN DO FOR YOU - THE DENTIST

Every culture since ancient times has used hypnosis to aid healing physically and emotionally. Through the latter part of the 1800s, hypnosis was readily accepted as an adjunct to medical treatments. Unfortunately, as chemical anesthesia became more sophisticated the use of hypnosis declined. Consequently, medical practitioners are often misinformed and unnecessarily skeptical about what hypnosis is and what it can accomplish.

However, an article entitled "Homeopathy, Herbs and Hypnosis: Common Practices in Complementary and Alternative Medicine," (*Jacksonville Medicine* January 2000) acknowledges:

> "Controlled experiments and clinical interventions document the ability of hypnotized individuals to control pain, reduce physiologic arousal in preparation for and during surgery, replace or supplement chemical anesthesia and analgesia and reduce bleeding, swelling, infection, post-operative complications and pain and reduce length of hospital stay. In dentistry, hypnosis is used for psychogenic oral pain, overcoming fear, gagging, tongue thrusting, thumb sucking, flow of saliva and capillary bleeding, bruxism, cooperation with procedures and as an anesthetic in place of chemical anesthesia due to allergies."

Consequently, dentists around the world are taking hypnosis more and more seriously. You may know that some of the first professionals to include hypnosis in their practice have been people like you- Dentists.

Hypnosis is a therapeutic approach with a scientific basis and with simple healing practices. Hypnosis is not voodoo and does not demean dental patients. It is easy to learn and apply, and saves you time and money when you become competent. Additionally, hypnosis supports the entire ethics of dentistry and many dentists are also trained hypnotists.

The goal of working with your consulting hypnotist, or using hypnosis yourself in your medical offices, is to enable and facilitate a ready, quick and painless treatment for patients.

– Hypnosis makes the dentist look good -

Pain management is only one way that hypnosis is useful in a medical/dental practice. Hypnosis has been used to successfully treat a wide range of conditions, including anxiety, eating disorders, phobias, fears, and addictive behaviors. Some of these issues you may want to deal with yourself and augment your dental income, however you will need to complete a certified hypnotist training. Others, you may wish to refer to a consulting hypnotist with whom you gain a working relationship. Some consulting hypnotists may welcome the opportunity to rent rooms from you three or four days a week which can increase your patient base and your referrals.

Dave Elman trained dentists and doctors in hypnosis and hypnoanalysis during the 1940's, 1950's and 1960's throughout the USA. His book, "Hypnotherapy", has a full chapter and many case histories of dentists using hypnosis successfully. As Dave says, "Suppose a man came into your office with an alarming gag reflex. A gag reflex is considered by most dentists well within the norm of human behavior. Not a complicated behavior pattern, but a quirk. No-one would think to send the patient to a psychiatrist because the patient is merely showing a peculiar reaction in a particular set of circumstances." In his book Elman says, "such a case yields itself to hypnoanalysis in five to ten minutes". Any other method would take weeks if not years meanwhile the patient's teeth deteriorate considerably.

Elman gives an example of a man who gagged and vomited. While in the hypnotic state of somnambulism, he went back to 1936 in WWII with carbon monoxide poisoning and having a long rubber tube inserted to wash out his stomach. Ever since, he had gagged and vomited when anything large came towards his mouth. Once his conscious mind could understand what his subconscious knew, the two minds could agree and the man never gagged again. Nowadays, thanks to Elman, these hypnoanalytical tools have been passed on through the teachings of instructors such as Gerald Kein and are available worldwide.

Extensive training is required to learn therapeutic hypnosis for use as a treatment or therapy. The consulting hypnotist learns how to induce a hypnotic state quickly and easily so that the subconscious and conscious minds agree and accept new ideas (i.e. suggestions) without resistance. However, the subject or patient must consent to accepting these suggestions and make the decision to let go of resistance.

WE would add that self-hypnosis techniques can easily be taught to patients so that they can manage pain or deal with other dental issues, such as habitual behaviors and fears that interfere with treatment protocols.

2. DENTISTS AND STRESS

When they go out socially and meet new people, dentists hear them say *"Ouch you're a dentist. I hate dentists".* In other words, what they are really saying is "I hate dental work being done on me" or "I have had a few bad experiences" or "the thought of dental work makes me cringe". Somehow, dentists have to learn not to take things personally. Your consulting hypnotist can help you be more relaxed when meeting such people..

There is also an urban myth that dentists have an unusually high suicide rate. This myth is based on an article by Steven Stack (2001) and the TV show *Seinfeld* also highlighted an episode to this belief.

Using 1990 data from 21 US states (covering 6198 suicides and 137,687 natural deaths, and taking demographic factors into account) Stack claimed that dentists had an odds ratio of 5.43 (compared to all the people in the sample). This is more than double the next group, doctors at a ratio of 2.31 (both the dentists' and the doctors' odds ratios were statistically significant).

It could be conjectured that dentists are "always down in the mouth..." or, as many now claim, that techniques and training have so improved that figures from 1990 need to be revisited. Indeed, since that report many states have included wellbeing courses in dental curricula.

Currently, statistics are difficult to collect and few states put occupation on their death certificates, so there is no US national data available on occupation related to suicide. Furthermore, Mr. Stack's findings are questioned by Roger E. Alexander, D.D.S., in "Stress Related Suicide by Dentists and Other Health Care Workers: Fact or Folklore" (*Journal of the American Dental Association June 2001*). Following a thorough review of the literature on dentists and suicide, Alexander concluded that Stack's analyses were "flawed by the use of hearsay, public perception, assumption, and currently outdated practice that may no longer be applicable". Yet, we understand that many dentists have heard this myth and may even believe it – and thus achieve it by worrying about it (a waking hypnotic response). This becomes a "law of attraction" and self-fulfilling unless the suggestion is eliminated.

In an article "Stress, Burnout, Anxiety and Depression among Dentists" Dr. Robert E. Rada, D.D.S., M.B.A. and Dr. Charmaine Johnson-Leong, B.D.S., M.B.A., the authors note many sources of professional stress encountered by dentists from dental school onwards: cash flow, practice management, societal issues, physical pain from standing and bending over. They find dentists are prone to professional burnout, anxiety disorders and clinical depression - not only a result of the nature of clinical practice but also "the personality traits commonly found among those who decide to pursue dental careers". Such disorders may affect dentists' personal relationships, professional relationships, health and well-being". Happily they conclude that "Treatment modalities and prevention strategies can help dentists conquer and avoid these disorders. The only limitation is their willingness to take care of themselves".

Happily, for the dentist, there is help for stress, professional burn-out and feelings of depression and being overwhelmed: The Consulting Hypnotist. When you learn self-hypnosis you can tune in to the "20 minute executive nap" at lunch time for relaxation and positive thinking. This can be done with a post hypnotic suggestion for self-hypnosis or by listening to a self-hypnosis CD. S/he can help you develop greater self-esteem, self-control and self-discipline as you learn to relax, see things in their true perspective and control your reaction to people, things and situations around you – as opposed to getting tense trying to control everything. In addition, referring your patients to a consulting hypnotist can relieve them of their tensions so when they arrive they, and consequently you, are able to work effectively and efficiently without emotional chaos. Some dentists take advantage of this by having a hypnotherapist as an associate working in their practices.

Contact your local hypnotists and ask for a free session to allow you to evaluate their services. Then you will begin to recognize those you can work with. Some may be qualified to train you in hypnotic techniques also. For a list of certified practitioners, contact National Accreditation bodies at the back of this book.

3. WHAT A CONSULTING HYPNOTIST CAN DO FOR YOUR PATIENTS

A consulting hypnotist can take the strain out of the job, for you and your patients.

Hypnosis for your patient has a wide range of applications including:

- Analgesia;
- Anesthesia;
- Anxiety and Fear (X-rays, needles, being leaned over etc.;)
- Bleeding from trauma to the lips or mouth;

- Bruxism;
- Control mouth opening
- Control of tongue movements
- Control of salivation
- Control of spasms of the jaw muscles
- Control sensations of the dental environment: equipment, sounds, smells, masks, gloves etc
- Control of body tension
- Control nausea
- Oral hygiene care and medication - Following instructions for follow up
- Placement of dentures
- Placement or adjustment of removable orthodontic appliances
- Placement of braces
- Phobia of injections
- Natural loss of baby teeth in children
- Hemostasis
- Smoking
- Thumb sucking
- TMJ

Some of the above can be done by simple suggestion, or even waking hypnosis. However, other long standing problems will need hypnoanalysis by a fully trained hypnotist involving techniques such as regression to cause and parts therapy.

The consulting hypnotist will work from your referral, and if required, come to your surgery or office and anesthetize patients there. A good way to check out their competency is to ask for a one to one consultation for yourself, check out their procedures and ethics, location and professional environment and certifications with up to date CEUs.

4.   WHAT THE DENTIST CAN DO WITH SIMPLE HYPNOTIC TECHNIQUES

There are simple techniques you, the dentist, can learn and use including waking hypnosis, NeuroLinguistic Programming (NLP) and language patterns, as well as learning formal hypnosis as an adjunct to your profession.

WAKING HYPNOSIS.

When a hypnotic effect is achieved without the use of formal hypnotic induction, such effects are called **waking hypnosis**. Example: It is summer time. You are extremely comfortable and enjoying the weather. Suddenly someone says, "Wow! It's hot!" In a moment or two, you notice that you are perspiring profusely. It does not occur to you that the suggestion precipitated "waking hypnosis," which brought on the perspiration. Every time a doctor gives or prescribes a placebo, s/he is using waking hypnosis.

The film ET provides a good example of how our brain processes affect our emotional state. When first shown in cinemas large numbers of the audience ended up in tears. Left brains were fully aware that we were watching a film about a model made of bits of wire and plastic, but our right brain said "yes, but he is dying" and we cry.

Try this experiment: In the presence of a number of people, crack open a perfectly fresh egg. Make a wry face and exclaim, *"Whew! This egg smells rotten. I wouldn't eat it for a thousand dollars."* Now, pass the egg around. Let everyone smell it. Some of the people present will agree that the perfectly fresh egg has an offensive odor. Some may even say it looks bad. When you have made the assertion, *"Whew! This egg smells rotten…",* you made a positive statement of apparent fact which your hearers accepted in total. You bypassed their critical factors, substituting your own. Respect for your judgment caused them to believe what you said even before they smelled the egg, thus minimizing their ability to judge the egg fairly.

So, people are readily suggestible without hypnosis, the mammoth advertising industry attests to that. People who are in hypnosis by definition, want to cooperate and they accept suggestions. They believe that shampoo is going to give them hair like the model on TV. They suspend their disbelief as they would while reading a novel, or listening to an authority figure such as a doctor, a dentist or a professor. But, if you suggest something that is distasteful to them. They will quickly stop cooperating.

Attaining Waking Hypnosis

"Waking suggestions" are given in a manner just like "hypnotic suggestions". Given with authority and confidence, they can produce strong changes. Experiments conducted by researchers such as Hull (1933) and subsequent research found a strong correlation between people's responses to suggestion both in and out of hypnosis.

For waking hypnosis to take place, certain conditions must take place:

1. The mind of the subject must lock itself around a given idea. This suggestion must not be objectionable to the subject. Suggestions must be given with complete confidence and absolute assurance. They must leave no room for doubt.

2. The suggestion must be one the patient wants – the suggestion must not be of objectionable to the subject. And, as the mind always wants to move from pain to pleasure, s/he is ready to hear any

suggestion of relief from someone who shows sympathy and understanding. For example; "Let's get you into my special relief chair where all that discomfort is going to be taken care of this morning. It will soon be a thing of the past. In fact it's probably feeling a lot better now that you're here, doesn't it?"

3. If the doubt creeps in, the suggestion becomes ineffective. Therefore, give suggestions in a manner that implies that what you have said is a certainty - with complete confidence and absolute assurance in words, tone and body language. LEAVE NO ROOM FOR DOUBT

4. In addition, for waking suggestion to be acceptable, the dentist needs to be in rapport with the patient. Building rapport can be somewhat difficult if the patient has white-coat syndrome, however your Consulting Hypnotist colleague can help with that. There are a number of techniques beneficial in building rapport for example, matching of non-verbal behavior (i.e., posture, gesture, breathing,).

Bandler and Grinder in their book "Structure of Magic" describe rapport and pacing well. While pacing, the practitioner just feeds back the client's current experience. Their approach is process oriented whereby the dentist would pace the ongoing experience of the client in order to build rapport and reduce resistance to the leading statements such as:

- You are sitting in that chair … (pacing)
- You are looking over here … (pacing)
- You are breathing in an even rhythm (pacing)
- Listening to the sound of my voice … (pacing)
- And as you move slightly in your chair … (pacing)
- You may also begin to find relaxation entering into an easy state of comfortableness … now, easily … (leading)
- And all the sounds in the room are here but just fading away as you lean back, now … (leading)

Waking Hypnosis can be an effective technique for easing and relaxing strong gag reflexes:

"I have a very simple method to help you with this (speak with authority and firmly). *I want you to focus your eyes right here – do not under any circumstance move your eyes from that (certificate on the wall) – I'm going to count from 1 – 5, and by the time I get to 5 all desire to gag, to reflux, in any way will disappear. 1-2-3-4-5 open your mouth please (and put tongue depressor in).*

Using a pencil or pen, you can use waking hypnosis which must be given with complete authority and power, no hesitation or body language of disbelief. In addition, the suggestion should not be objectionable to the person.

"Put this pencil in your hand like this .... hold it with steady and firm pressure on that pencil. Not uncomfortable, just steady now. And, do you know the most interesting thing is going to happen. As long as you hold that pencil in your left hand, As long as you keep up this pressure, gentle but firm, you're going to discover that you have absolutely no desire or inclination to gag. Gagging is totally eliminated from now on .... So just continue to hold on to that pencil now & notice how comfortably you feel relaxed, calm confident and in control. You're In control of your reactions and at ease. Breathing through your nose is easy for you, easily and effortlessly taking in good clean air remaining calm, confident and in control.

You reinforce the suggestion, once in a while during treatment by saying:

"As you continue to hold the pencil, I want you to visualize, picture, or imagine that as I'm treating you, you will feel calm and relaxed at all times while you focus on the pencil."

It's ALL bypass of the critical factor!

GUIDELINES FOR DEVELOPING RAPPORT AND WAKING HYPNOSIS

1. **Introduce Yourself:** as it takes away worry on how to address you later. For example: "Hi my name is Thomas, you must be Brian James. Let's go and talk about any concerns you may have about being here today." If accompanied by a friend or family member then greet them also and ask if they wish to accompany you both. Now you can ask "Shall I call you Brian or Mr. James?" Remember to introduce your assistant also, even allow them to chat e.g. about weather, the parking or whatever.

2. **Reassure the Fearful:** Ask your patient, "How are you feeling right now?". Reassure them; "fearing dental treatment is quite normal, you know we're not supposed to like it! It is just something we have to do, and just get on with it. Nothing to be ashamed of. In fact I used to be scared until I understood it more and more – now it's easy for me".

3. **Explain what to expect** and suggest that any sensations they feel are perfectly acceptable. You want to reduce fear of the unknown so describe what the sensation will feel like. Avoid using the word

"pain" and use the phrase "a little discomfort" (the sensation is no longer perceived as frightening and unpleasant.

4. **Match your words and body language** and the patient will believe your body language first. With this in mind, it is essential that your posture, facial expression and tone of voice do not conflict with the words you choose.

5. **Smile and greet the patient** in the neutral reception area before walking with them to the treatment room as it is seen as a personal commitment to caring for them.

6. **Maintain eye contact** and it demonstrates you are sincere, interested in them and honest. Constant eye contact may feel uncomfortable so ask the patient if they mind you taking notes as you chat then you can glance towards those occasionally.

7. **Sound calm, confident and in control at all times**. A high-pitched squeaky voice will appear immature while a fast voice can elicit fear. So breathe and match the patient's rhythm as the patient gradually slows down until they will pace you..

8. **Be enthusiastic** for it inspires confidence in you. Tell patients about similar procedures you have done previously, and describe how well the patients are now doing. Keep talking about the end result during the treatment and how great they are going to feel. This helps them stay motivated and wanting to please you.

9. **Agree to a hand signal** which the patient can use to signal if they become uncomfortable. I (Beryl) just smack my thigh twice and my dentist moves away, I take water and spit, then lie back in the chair. I have not had to do that for many years but just reminding him each time I lie back helps me feel more comfortable and in control as I go into my self-hypnosis.

10. **A steady flow of reassuring chat** can be helpful and distract your patient as something different to focus upon.

11. **A Good Dental Assistant** can give help and allow you to concentrate on a more complicated procedure. They can also help if you say "the wrong thing" or become irritated. "I'm just going to ask Susan to finish up cleaning with the floss, and you will see she has the gentlest hands ever". Hearing you working well together as a team is very reassuring.

12. **Sounds Around:** *"All the sounds around just help you relax much more. You may feel as if you hear some creaking noises as the tooth starts to move, and this is a GOOD thing as it tells us things are going according to plan and we are nearly finished".*

13. **Handle Gently and with Permission:** Patients talk to others about how you handle them. *"My dentist is the gentlest in town, I feel so safe". "You're lucky. Mine pushes and pulls, she never says what she's going to do next – give me the name of your dentist, I am going to call her".* I know which one you want to be! If you are going to prod or probe, ask for permission. They will accept more discomfort when they have given permission. A gentle touch on the shoulder becomes a reassuring anchor - carefully observe the patient's reaction though to make sure they are comfortable with contact in this way.

14. **Be Honest:** The more trust your patient has in you, the less fearful they are. Gaining rapport and trust takes time yet can be lost in a moment. Once lost it may never be fully recovered. If a procedure is going to be uncomfortable, say so but use language to encourage the patient to believe that the discomfort will be acceptable e.g. *"it may feel a bit like a paper scratch on your finger initially ouch then just a "there" feeling. OK?"*

15. **Tag Questions:** such as: "that's OK isn't it", you're feeling better already aren't you?" and accompany with positive imagery. When the Protective Factor of the Subconscious Mind has information it can respond, and it responds best to the language of imagery. *"I am going to do X, and Y may happen when it does that's a good sign we are on our way to getting this over and sometimes it does Z which is just another way for the tooth to react, and just as good. Is that OK with you?" You can do that can't you?"* With rising intonation and the patient nods, you have some trance work going on.

16. **Simple Non-Threatening Language** i.e. using everyday words for your apparatus and avoiding words like "cut" or slice" to "I'll just be working in this area here for a while and you relax deeply as we go deeper into the back tooth just around here easily and naturally breathing, in, and, out now. There we are. This is good isn't it?"

17. **Post Treatment Praise:** *"You did really well today Sally. And that's going to be even easier for you next time, to relax more and more easily. Aren't you proud of yourself?"*

THE IMPORTANCE OF LANGUAGE

Hypnosis is "the bypass of the critical factor" our **words, body language and tone of voice** send messages directly to the subconscious mind and we react. There are powerful words which the dentist can use (and others to avoid) in order to change the patient's reality.

Words to avoid: include negatives e.g. don't. won't, can't – as in "this won't hurt" and the mind actually begins to imagine a hurt ... "don't worry" and the mind begins to wonder what they should worry about. Avoid using "don't" and "but" which can signal to the brain to beware of impending negativity.

Better ways to say this would be

o *"Some people feel a little discomfort. You can deal with a little discomfort can't you?"* and *"remember a time when you dealt with some discomfort, how you felt that in your body ... ..."*

o Use comparative words (more, better, best, greatest) where one or both of the objects compared is unspecified: *"The more you practice being here in this chair, the better you will become at relaxing."*

o Use quantifying words: all, every, everyone, for example: *"You can always improve your relaxation with every session we have." "Many people feel really good once that tooth is out and gone and it's over, so let's focus on that now, and relax"*

o *"Before you go into trance, I'd like you to sit comfortably in that chair as we talk about your dental outcomes for today."*

o *"When you go into trance, you may discover new levels of relaxation that you didn't realize you had yet".*

o *"Remember how good you felt after your last tooth extraction and focus on that great feeling now, as you relax into this chair easily and effortlessly".*

Instead of	Use
drill	hand piece
surgery	consultation room
waiting room	lounge, or seating area
pain	discomfort, or a little uncomfortable
inject anesthetic	let the anesthetic soak in r-e-a-l-l-y slowly
I'll try to	I am going to
extract a tooth	remove a tooth
tooth extraction	tooth removal
but, however	and
pull	ease out
This may hurt	Just a little discomfort now

Script Suggestion for drills' (hand piece) sounds

"No matter what type of sounds you hear wonderful relaxation taking you deeper and deeper, drifting drift away from external sounds, all sounds around help and guide you deeper and deeper, relaxed. The sound you are interested in is the sound of my voice and the sound of my voice always helps you relax, easily... now". The sound of equipment, hand held devices, squirters and drills sounds of no concern or importance to you, no concern of yours whatsoever"

5. SIX STEPS TO HYPNOSIS IN THE DENTAL CHAIR

STEP ONE: RAPPORT & PRE-TALK

Your patient's biggest concerns are anxiety, apprehension, for some: terror. Greet the patient outside the treatment room and put them at ease first before moving into the treatment room with all its strange smells and instruments. Having a great assistant in reception that is sensitive and can put people at ease is a great bonus.

The only thing that can stop hypnosis taking place is fear of hypnosis or distrust of the practitioner

- Answer all questions with truth and confidence.
- Explain what will be done and how they will feel during hypnosis
- Explain hypnosis as natural – answer their questions.
- Discuss that "trying" too much can get in the way.
- Have client visit the bathroom first!
- Have client write their benefits, suggestions before they come.
- Become a walking, talking example of how hypnosis works.
- Have a professional environment.
- Only tackle in hypnosis what you have conscious permission to do.
- Maybe give a recording to listen to before next session.
- Practice on friends.
- If you plan to use the word sleep – then explain how you mean the word.
- Do not make guarantees of success – explain the success of your clients and others and explain barriers to success honestly.

- Switch off phones.
- Cover exposed flesh – ladies may feel "exposed" if wearing skimpy clothing so have a lightweight blanket available.
- Give an estimate of number of sessions required from the beginning.
- Personal appearance should be professional.
- Listen – but do not believe what you are told, and never argue. Remember they are only telling you what they know from their conscious mind.

  ✍ **You must educate your clients during the pre-talk!** ✍

STEP TWO: INDUCTION

The two most important preliminary steps for a successful induction are:

1. Enhance the client's imagination.
2. Create mental expectancy.

   - What the mind expects to happen tends to be realized. Build the client's mental expectancy and the instant induction will work every time!
   - Hypnosis is simply the bypass of the critical factor of the conscious mind and the establishment of acceptable selective thinking.

Rapid and Instant Inductions

Rapid Induction is an induction done in around 4 minutes, it has built in testers

Instant Inductions are exactly that, often seen in stage shows when the hypnotist says "sleep!"

The use of instantaneous and rapid inductions enhances your practice and can eliminate many problems that come up with some clients.

Some of the problems that can be eliminated are:

- None of your tired late afternoon or evening clients will go to sleep on you before doing the suggestion work. This frequently happens when using a progressive relaxation induction.
- Testing is built into many of the inductions; which can create awareness by your client that s/he is indeed in hypnosis. This eliminates the "I don't think I was hypnotized" syndrome.

- You will have more time for actual transformational therapy. If you only use 1 minute or less on the induction, instead of 15-30 minutes, your client will benefit greatly from the increased therapy time.

Steps to the Instant Induction

1. *Get permission: "You do want to go into hypnosis don't you?"*
2. Create a rapid unexpected movement of some part or all *of* the client's body. This creates the bypass of the critical factor by overloading the nervous system.
3. Fire in the suggestion, "sleep!" As the client's energy level drops down, he drops into trance.
4. Immediately say to the client, "I've got you. Let every muscle go loose, limp and relaxed."

Elman Hand Drop Instant Induction: by Gerald F. Kein

"Place your hand in mine…. Like that – got it?

Now, look at me – right here (point to forehead)

At the count of three, press down continuously against my hand.

I'll be pressing up against your power …… got it?

Now, follow my instructions completely…. Ok?

One (wagging your finger at the subject with each count)

Two, three….. Push, push, push. That's right ….. Push hard, that's good.

Now, let your eyes become heavy, droopy,,, drowsy and sleepy …. Closing, ……closing…….

(if you have to, pull the subject's eyelids shut with your thumb and index finger.)

(now, instantly pull your hand out from under the subject's and say "sleep" and tap the subject on the forehead with the palm of your hand.)

As I rock your head gently, allow your body to go loose and limp and deeply relaxed. Every breath guiding you deeper relaxed.

As I lift your head allow the movement to guide you deeper relaxed and allow your neck to hold your head quite comfortably.

(do a five to one count down for eye catalepsy then
fractionation and check for somnambulism)

Script: The Dave Elman Induction (Elman Rapid Induction)

*Now take a long deep breath and hold it for a few seconds. And another, and as you exhale this breath, allow your eyes to close and **let go of the surface tension in your body**. Just let your body relax as much as possible, right now.*

*Now, place your **awareness on your eye muscles** and relax the muscles around your eye; all the little muscles that work so hard all day. See every fiber and every cell relaxing, relaxing around every muscle ….to the point they just won't work. When you're sure they are so relaxed that as long as you hold on to this relaxation, they just won't work, hold on to that relaxation and test them to make sure THEY WON'T WORK. Stop Testing now as all sounds and distractions fade away and allow them to take you deeper relaxed now*

*And, this relaxation you have in your eyes is the **same quality of relaxation** that I want you to have throughout your whole body. So, just let this quality of relaxation flow, now, through your whole body from the top of your head, to the tips of your toes. Imagine a warm blanket of relaxation surrounding you, with each and every breath you take.*

*1) Now, we can **deepen this relaxation much more**. In a moment, I'm going to have you open and close your eyes. When you close your eyes, that's your signal to let this feeling of relaxation become 10 times deeper. All you have to do is want it to happen and you can make it happen very easily. Ok, now, open your eyes….now close your eyes and feel that relaxation flowing through your entire body, taking you much, much deeper. Use your wonderful imagination, and imagine your whole body is covered, and wrapped, in a warm blanket of total peace and relaxation.*

*2) Now, we can **deepen this relaxation much more**. In a moment, I'm going to have you open and close your eyes one more time. Again, when you close your eyes, double the relaxation you now have. Make it become twice as deep. Ok, now once more, open your eyes….close your eyes and double your relaxation……good. Let every muscle in your body become so relaxed that as long as you hold on to this quality of relaxation, every muscle of your body will not work.*

*3) In a moment, I'm going to have you open and close your eyes one more time. Again, when you close your eyes, **double the relaxation you now have**. Make it become twice as deep. Ok, now, once more, open your eyes…..close your eyes and double your relaxation…..good. Let every muscle in your body become so relaxed that as long as you* *hold on to this quality of relaxation, every muscle of your body will not work.*

*In a moment, I'm going to **lift your (right/ left) hand by the wrist**, just a few inches, and drop it. If you have followed my instructions up to this point that hand will be so relaxed it will be just as loose and limp as a wet dish cloth and will simply plop down. Each time, now, don't try to help me, you have to remove relaxation. Let me do all the lifting so that when I release it, it just plops down and you'll allow yourself to go much deeper.* (subject helps to lift the hand say,) *"No, no let me do all the lifting. Don't help me. Let it be heavy. Let me take the weight. You'll feel it when you have it.*

*You've done a wonderful job relaxing, that's complete physical relaxation. I want you to know that there are **two ways a person can relax**. You can relax physically and you can relax mentally. You already proved that you can relax physically, now let me show you how to relax mentally. In a moment, I'll ask you to begin slowly counting backwards, out loud, from 100. Now, here's the secret to mental relaxation. With each number you say, say the words deeper relaxed and double your mental relaxation. With each number you say, let your mind become twice as relaxed as you say "deeper relaxed" let the numbers fade. Now if you do this, by the time you reach the number 96, or maybe even sooner, your mind will have become so relaxed, you will have actually relaxed everything out of your mind that would have come after 96, right out of your mind.*

Hypnotherapist	Client
"Now, begin, and double your mental relaxation."	*100*
"Now double that mental relaxation. Let everything already start to fade. Push them out"	*99*
"Double your mental relaxation. Start to make everything leave. *They'll go if you will them away."*	*98*
"Now, they'll be gone. Dispel them. Banish them. Make it happen. You can."	*97*

*As I told you, you will always be **aware of the sounds around you**. You are not asleep, just relaxed, you can cough, you can speak, scratch your nose if you want to! The only difference is that from this moment on, any sounds you hear will not affect or disturb you in any way......As a matter of fact, any sounds you hear (examples) will just help and guide you to go deeper relaxed. The only sound you remain interested in is the **sound of my voice** and the sound of my voice always helps you to relax much more. Everything you think, do and say will allow you* *to continue moving deeper into a wonderful depth of trance where you can be successful with your goals for this session today.*

Eye Closure Test: *Imagine water on your eyes, super glued together: Try in vain to open your eyes but you can't. The more you try to open your eyes you can't. Can't open your eyes, you can't. But you want to, but you can't, you can't, try, try but you can't.*

STEP THREE: DEEPENING

We want to deepen the patient to a state of somnambulism. Methods for deepening include:

1. Periods of silence... Suggest, *"until I again touch you on the shoulder, you will continue to go deeper and deeper relaxed. You will pay no attention to my voice."* Do not leave the subject alone longer than 15 or 20 minutes, for some subjects tend to come out of hypnosis on their own or lapse into a normal sleep.

2. Exhaling... Suggest, *"each time you exhale, you will automatically sink deeper."* I usually combine this suggestion with a period of silence.

3. Counting... Counting up or counting down from any number, i.e., 10-1. I prefer to count down because it lends to the feeling of sinking deeper.

4. Hallucination... Walking steps, riding in a car or train, sailing, going in a tunnel or down a corridor, sliding, etc. Combine counting with hallucinations adds to the effect, i.e., riding down an elevator, going down one floor with each count.

5. Ideo-motor suggestions... Eye catalepsy, arm catalepsy, etc.

6. Ideo-sensory suggestions. . Hot and cold sensations, and those affecting the senses, sound, touch, smell and taste.

7. Pyramiding... Repeated inductions without awakening.

8. Fractionation... Hypnotizing, dehypnotizing and rehypnotizing several times.

9. Indirect suggestions... While the subject is hypnotized, direct your suggestions to someone else. Explain what is happening and what is going to happen. Thus, the subject indirectly receives the suggestions.

10. Feedback... Sensations which the subject feels are fed back to him.

11. Placebo... Pill, drink, *harmless* certain procedures, which the subject believes will affect him.

12. Compounding suggestions... Suggest that every move they make and every suggestion you give sends them deeper relaxed.

13. Post-hypnotic suggestions... To respond to a signal, to go deeper each time they are hypnotized, etc.

14. Realization… Bringing it to their attention, that the effect is working, and that they are responding.

Example of ideo-sensory suggestions deepening:

*"As I told you, you will always be aware of the sounds around you. You are not asleep, just relaxed. The only difference is that from this moment on, any sound you hear will not affect or disturb you in any way. As a matter of fact, any sounds you hear, (**mention any ones they might hear**) will just help and guide you to go deeper relaxed. The only sound you remain interested in is the sound of my voice and the sound of my voice always helps you to relax much more. Following my suggestions is easy and following my voice and the words I say helps you, relax, go deeper."*

STEP FOUR: TEST FOR DEPTH

You want to make sure your patient is in a state of either somnambulism, analgesia for light dental, or anesthesia i.e. the Esdaile State (for achieving this deeper level we advise hypnotherapy training and practice).

There are several outward signs of somnambulistic trance that can be observed in all subjects. These signs cannot be simulated by the subject. The subject will exhibit at least one, and in many cases, multiple signs:

1. Body warmth: Many subjects note a distinct change in body temperature. Many subjects feel cold, and others feel warm. This is attributed to the lower pulse rate and extreme relaxation of the subject.

2. Fluttering eyelids: Virtually all subjects in trance exhibit a 'fluttering of eyelids'. The subject is actually in R. E. M. state. (Rapid Eye Movement)

3. Reddening of the eyes: All subjects will demonstrate a reddening of the eyes once they have entered trance. This phenomenon is attributed to the relaxation of the muscles in the eyes of the subject, allowing a greater flow of blood through the veins.

4. Increased lacrimation: Many subjects, upon entering trance, will exhibit an increased 'tearing of the eyes.' This is attributed to the relaxation of the muscles surrounding the tear ducts.

5. Eyes rolling back: Many, upon entering trance, experience their eyes rolling back in their head. It will appear as if the subject is looking up through the top of his head.

Test for Somnambulism 1 - Analgesia

(The following technique is used as a test or challenge in order to show the client that s/he has experienced hypnosis. The following wording will take this technique far beyond a simple test.)

"With nothing …. but wonderful thoughts and beautiful feelings throughout your entire body now. .. I am going to lightly touch your right hand. As I touch your right hand, you will become aware of a numbing sensation. The right hand is becoming more and more numb. I am now lifting the right hand up into the air, and it feels wonderful. (You may now use either Option #1 or Option #2 listed below.)

Option #1 - *As you being to notice the change in your right hand, I would like you to nod your head "yes" and relax even further. As you feel the numbing sensation, nod your head "yes", and relax.*

Option #2 - Dentist pinches client's hand with fingernails to the point that there will be a mark after the session is complete. This serves as a convincer that they were in hypnosis.

The same part of your powerful mind that was able to make your hand become numb is now causing a numbing sensation directed at _____. Yes, you are creating a numbing sensation for _____. You will be successful in every way. Enjoy this success".

Test for Somnambulism 2 - Analgesia

"Now I'm going to pick up your arm again. I'm going to rub the back of your hand here and make this particular spot here, as I'm rubbing it, analgesic. As you know, analgesia removes the sense of discomfort, as compared to anesthesia, which removes the sense of touch completely. I'm making the spot analgesic, no sense of discomfort. You may feel a pleasant numb feeling, but in any case, a complete removal of the sense of pain or discomfort. (Pinch a spot on their hand). *Very good. Deep relaxation".*

Test beyond Somnambulism - Number Block

"I'm going to ask you in a moment to please count to ten slowly. When I say ready, I want you to count out loud, very slowly, form one to ten. Ready, please begin counting. (Subject counts.)

Very good, now I'm going to ask you to count again in a moment; however, this time there is nothing between five and seven. Even if you think of something between five and seven, you'll be unable to articulate it, unable to speak it. Nothing between five and seven. You'll count: 1 –

2 –3 - 4 – 5 -   - 7 – 8 – 9 - 10. What was there between 5 and 7 has gone, erased.

Please count aloud, slowly, again for me. (Patient counts*). Very good, this is the way you count, nothing between five and seven. Well done,* (lift their hand and drop) *Go deeper".*

STEP FIVE: SUGGESTION   (for Regression/Therapy Work followed by Suggestions ... see section for hypnotists)

Glove Anesthesia (following this suggestion you will do your light dental work)

The first thing that I would like you to do is to raise one of your hands up to about your chin height. Focus your attention on the hand that you raised. Feel the sensations in that hand. Imagine a tingling sensation begin with the little finger on that hand. You can even separate the fingers slightly and raise the little finger up above the others, as if in old English times and holding a cup of tea. Imagine a tingling sensation beginning in that finger. As if it was electrically charged or about to go to sleep. We all know how that feels, when we have slept on top of a hand and it feels numb the next morning isn't that right? This is the same sensation.

There is a pulsing, tingling sensation in that finger. Your little finger is becoming quite numb and the numb feeling spreads to the ring finger... raise the ring finger up too. It tingles, feeling funny. Again the numbness spreads and the third finger feels numb, too. Tingling or feeling a course of electricity through it. Nod your head if you know what I mean . . . Good. Now the next finger, in fact all the fingers on that hand feel tingly. The tingle spreads to the palm and back of the hand. Take a moment, breathe, and as you exhale notice the feelings as the hand is beginning to feel numb. You can even take your other hand and tap gently on the back of this one.

You are feeling for numb spots as you gently drum your fingers on the back of the hand that we have been focusing on. When you can numb your hand, you can transfer this numbness to any other part of your body. Do that now, for example, on your thigh, your leg. Place the numb hand on your leg and just imagine as if the tingling feeling is transferring to that leg. In just a few moments it will begin to feel numb. This is all quite natural and easy, and you feel very comfortable all the while. You may feel some pressure, but no discomfort. The memory of the hand falling asleep is being activated in your mind right now.

It is producing the response. Your mind knows how to facilitate these changes. Each time that you practice this, you will find the numbing response is five times faster than the last time. It is five times easier to reproduce, five times quicker, every time that you practice. You are training that part of your mind to interact with you and bring this phenomenon forth. It is quite natural, quite comfortable, and quite easy for you. So let's do that now.

Numb your hand. Transfer this numbness to your thigh, your leg. Place the numb hand on your leg and just imagine as if the tingling feeling is transferring to that leg. In just a few moments it will begin to feel numb. This is all quite natural and easy, and you feel very comfortable all the while. You may feel some pressure, but no discomfort. The memory of the hand falling asleep is being activated in your mind right now. Place the numb hand on your (right) cheek and just imagine as if the tingling feeling is transferring to that cheek and mouth area. In just a few moments, it will begin to feel numb. Down through the entire cheek, all the way to the gum area here the teeth and roots of the teeth. That's right, all the way down deeper and deeper. Nod your head when you've got that. (Repeat for last two paragraphs for left cheek, chin upper teeth.)

Post Hypnotic Convincer: Color Red

There are three reasons why this technique may be used often:

1. It works to reinforce the post-hypnotic suggestion.
2. The client realizes that they have been hypnotized.
3. The success of the technique is instant.

"You will find that over the next few days the color red is going to seem brighter, sharper, and more noticeable. The color red could be a car's tail-light, color of a car, stop light, clothing. It could be as small as a lady's nail polish, or as large as a billboard, or simply a card. The color red, red, red will seem brighter, sharper, and more noticeable than ever before. ..... . Each time your mind encounters the color red, your feelings of wellness and comfort in dental procedures with me will become stronger. You like keeping your teeth clean and you return for regular treatment. You will not need to look for the color red, you will notice it automatically."

STEP SIX: EMERGE

Some people like to think of this as "awakening" however, we prefer to call this stage emerging. The patient is emerging from a natural state - they have not been asleep! It is a good time to reinforce and use compounding of suggestions of wellbeing while emerging. These suggestions are designed to reinforce and summarize the newly acquired beliefs, integrating the new behaviors so that they become a reality in the future. For example, suggest that each session will be ten times more powerful and effective as the one before.

While emerging is a good time to embed suggestions for time distortion e.g. *"even though we have spent a few minutes today doing hypnosis, you have found it to be very beneficial, a beneficial experience for you."*

If a client will not emerge that is because they really like being in the state and you could either leave them to continue into sleep (good for pain relief) or use **the "coma threat"** i.e. *"I know you love this wonderful state of deep relaxation, it's great and you can go back any time you choose. However, I want you to know that unless you come out by the time I count number five now, you will NEVER be able to achieve this wonderful state of hypnosis ever again. And in emerging now you make it easier and easier to go into hypnosis with a trained person any time you choose. Okay now 1.. 2.. 3.. 4.. 5*

Finally, present post-hypnotic suggestions. When clients open their eyes they remain open to suggestion so be positive and compound suggestions e.g. suggest they had a good experience in hypnosis.

They often emerge thirsty. It is a good sign of hypnosis having taken place. Reassure them of this and so offer a glass of water to help the patient become more alert. It is a great reinforcing suggestion also as, for a few minutes they are remain susceptible to suggestion. So as they open their eyes you may say' *"you look like you needed that! You're probably feeling a little thirsty right now. Have a sip of water and notice how good you feel"*

Emerging script 1

If you counted your patient into hypnosis with a count down, then emerge with a count up (and vice versa)

"Each time that you use this hypnosis method for easy relaxation, you relax more easily, more quickly, and more deeply. Relaxation is a skill that you are easily developing with trance.

Now, I'm going to count from one to five, and then I'll say, "Fully aware." At the count of five, your eyes are open, and you are then fully aware, feeling calm, rested, refreshed, and relaxed. All right.

One: slowly, calmly, easily you're returning to your full awareness once again.

Two: each muscle, nerve in your body is loose and limp, and relaxed, and you feel wonderfully good.

Three: from head to toe, you are feeling perfect in every way. Physically perfect; mentally perfect; emotionally calm and serene.

On the number four, your eyes begin to feel sparkling clear. On the next number I count, eyelids open, fully aware, feeling calm, rested, refreshed, relaxed, invigorated, and full of energy.

Number five: You're fully aware now. Eyelids open. Take a good, deep breath, fill up your lungs, and stretch. "

Emerging script 2   (this example presumes you counted forward to hypnotize them so it is counting down accordingly. Adjust is you count down for hypnosis and up for emergence)

We have now finished our session. You will carry with you all of the new behavior patterns you have learned, as well as a sense of well-being. I will count from 5 to 1, allowing you to slowly return to full alertness, leaving your safe place with the confidence that you will be able to return to it anytime you want.

Let's begin: 5 ...beginning to drift back to complete alertness; 4 ...closer now to complete awareness; 3 ...becoming aware of your surroundings; 2 ... feeling refreshed and rejuvenated; and 1.

When you feel ready to return to your day, looking forward to your dental visits, open your eyes, and look forward to positive results from this hypnosis session. You feel refreshed, rejuvenated, and ready.

Script: Emerge with preparation for instant hypnosis next time

"In a few moments...when I count up to 'FIVE "...you will open your eyes....and be wide awake again. You will emerge feeling wonderfully better for this long sleep. You will come back feeling completely relaxed.....both mentally and physically....feeling quite calm and composed........ with more energy and vitality than you have had for a long time.

In a few moments...when I count up to 'seven"...you will open your eyes....and be wide awake again. You will be back feeling wonderfully better for this long sleep. You will feel completely relaxed......mentally and physically....feeling quite calm and composed.

From now on.....you will never have to wait to go into this wonderful state of relaxation again. You will not need a long induction into hypnosis.

From now on....whenever you want me to give you treatment....all I shall have to do is ask you to lie back comfortably....and look straight at me. While you are looking at me....I shall say: Go to sleep!

And from now on....whenever you hear me say......'Go to sleep' Your eyes will always close immediately.....and you will always fall immediately into a sleep....just as deep as this one.

It doesn't matter whether it is tomorrow…..next week….next month….or even next year. From now on….whenever you hear me say….'Go to sleep'……Your eyes will always close immediately…..and you will always fall immediately into a sleep….just as deep as this one.

And that is exactly what is going to happen when you come to see me next. After our preliminary chat…..as soon as you are ready for treatment….

I shall ask you to lay back comfortably in the chair….and look straight at me. While you are looking at me….I shall say: Go to sleep!

And next time……and, indeed, on every future occasion when you want me to give you treatment….the moment you hear me say….'Go to sleep"…your eyes will close immediately….and you will fall immediately into a sleep….just as deep as this one".

HYPNOSIS IN DENTAL SCHOOLS

An abbreviated version (compared to the National Guild of Hypnotists CH course) of HypnoDontics was first taught in dental schools in North America in 1948 as part of the regular curriculum until the early 60's. Currently, privately operated schools along with both colleges and universities still offer dental hypnosis, but on a post-graduate basis, involving 2 - 3 day courses covering basic information and techniques.

With the cost of setting up a practice, training and remunerating staff, insurance, maintaining pharmaceutical supplies, financing and updating computer and dental software and hardware, running and maintaining office water lines, etc., the working dentist is more concerned with paying bills by practicing dentistry proper rather than extending themselves into a sub-specialty that isn't generally covered by patient insurance.

Take into consideration that the decline of hypnosis included in the dental school curriculums was not due to any lack of confidence in the effectiveness of the hypnotic method, but was due to the more measurable reliability of chemical anesthetics vs. hypnosis, which have remained.

Lists of some courses offered for dentists and dental care practitioners are listed in the appendix.

Section 4
Working with Children

In this section we will look at issues to do with dentistry and children:

1. **Children and Dentistry**
   - **Formation of teeth**
   - **Pregnancy**
   - **Infancy**
   - **Childhood**
   - **Teens**

2. **Children and Hypnosis**

3. **Scripts for Working with Children**

1. CHILDREN AND DENTISTRY

It is necessary for the consulting hypnotist to understand basics of the world of dentistry in order to converse with the dentist and understand their patients' requirements in order to make suggestions consistent with good dental health.

Uses of Teeth

- Teeth help in chewing of food.
- Teeth help in phonation *(the utterance of sounds)*
- They offer support to the facial tissues and therefore are important in facial appearance.
- Presence of teeth helps maintain the health of the jaws.

Milk Teeth and Permanent Teeth

Humans exhibit two sets of teeth. At birth, no teeth are visible. Soon, primary or the milk teeth appear in the oral cavity. These primary teeth are later shed off and are replaced by the permanent teeth.

Parts of a Tooth

The human tooth has two primary components: the crown and root. The crown is the portion of the tooth that projects above the gums while the root is that portion that anchors the tooth to the bone.

The teeth are composed of 4 tissues.

1. The **enamel** covers the crown of the teeth and is the hardest known substance in the human body. This extreme hardness is necessary to survive the powerful forces exerted on the tooth surface during chewing.

2. Inner to the enamel is the **dentin** forming the bulk of the tooth.

3. **Cementum** covers the **root** portion of the tooth and gives attachment to certain fibers called **periodontal ligaments** that help the tooth attach to the jaws.

4. The **pulp** is the innermost part of the tooth containing the nerves, blood vessels and other cells. The pulp is the vital area of the tooth. **Gums** are soft tissues that cover the tooth like a collar.

Arrangement of Teeth

Teeth are embedded in the upper and lower jaw bones. They are arranged in each jaw in the form of an arch. When we close our mouths, the teeth of the upper and lower arches interdigitate with one another. This in scientific words is called **occlusion.**

Types of Teeth

Humans have teeth of four distinct types, each having a typical appearance and performing a certain function.

1. The **incisors** are the front teeth that are so called because they help to incise food. They are flat blade-like teeth. There are 2 incisors in each quadrant of the jaw.(8 total)

2. **Canines** (cuspids) are teeth that are present at the corners of the mouth. They are pointed teeth that help in shearing food. (4 total)

3. Next to the canines are 2 **premolars**, (also referred to as bicuspids) which have broader grinding surfaces and therefore help in chewing and grinding food. (8 total)

4. The **molars** are the large back teeth having large grinding surfaces used primarily to grind food. (8 total plus 4 wisdom teeth-3rd molars)

PREGNANCY

Does a Pregnant Woman's Diet Affect Her Child's Teeth

Prevention of dental problems should ideally start during pregnancy. The pregnant woman should have a wholesome and nutritious diet that would help in proper development of the growing fetus.

The expectant mother should also have a diet that is rich in calcium to ensure the healthy development of the baby's bones and teeth.

Good sources of calcium are cheese, milk, yogurt, leafy vegetables and dairy products. A good diet during pregnancy ensures to yield healthy teeth and bones in the child.

Medicines Taken During Pregnancy

There are certain medicines and antibiotics that should be avoided during pregnancy. These drugs can cause defective development of the developing fetus.

Tetracycline antibiotics, when consumed by pregnant women cause permanent brownish grey staining of the child's teeth. Thus, self-medication should be avoided during pregnancy, and other medicines should be taken only after consultation with the physician.

INFANCY

When Should an Infant First Visit the Dentist

It is a good idea to consult the dentist by six months of age when the first milk teeth are expected to emerge into the oral cavity. Regular visits to the dentist every 6 months will help in giving adequate preventive care to the child that will aid in preventing dental decay. If there are any cavities, it is good to undertake the treatment at an early stage.

These regular visits are advised even if you think the baby's teeth are healthy. These regular visits also help the child get used to the idea of a fun visit to the dentist before they need any treatment to be administered.

What Are Milk Teeth?

Humans have two sets of teeth. The teeth that appear first are called the milk teeth, **deciduous dentition**, baby teeth or the primary teeth. These teeth are later shed off and are replaced by a permanent set of teeth called the **permanent dentition**. They are called Milk Teeth as they resemble the color of milk, and are whiter than the permanent teeth that replace them.

When Do Teeth Start Appearing?

The milk teeth normally start appearing at 6 months of age, give or take a few months earlier or later. The first milk teeth to appear are the lower front teeth, called the lower central incisor. However, the order of eruption of different teeth may vary in some children.

It is quite normal for the teeth to erupt 3-6 months later than the expected time. However, delay beyond 6 months may be an indication that you should consult your dentist, who will try determining the cause of the delay.

What are Natal and Neonatal Teeth?

Rarely are babies born with teeth, but teeth that are seen at birth are called natal teeth, while teeth that appear within a month of birth are called neonatal teeth. These teeth are retained unless they are very mobile or pose major problems in nursing.

At What Age Do the Milk Teeth Shed?

Although the milk teeth erupt by 3 years of age, they are shed from 6 years onwards until about 10 years of age and the permanent teeth start appearing by 6 years of age. Between the ages of 6 - 9 years the child has some milk teeth as well as some permanent teeth. This period is called the mixed dentition period. By about 12 years old, all the milk teeth should be shed off and replaced by the permanent teeth.

Why Do Milk Teeth Become Mobile?

As the permanent teeth start emerging they wear off the roots of the milk teeth. Thus, the milk teeth lose their support in the bone and become mobile. The milk teeth are ultimately shed off and are replaced by the permanent teeth.

Are Spaces Between Teeth Normal in Children?

Yes. These spaces between the teeth help later in accommodating the bigger permanent teeth. The absence of spaces between the milk teeth in children may be a forewarning that the child may not have adequate space to accommodate the bigger permanent teeth, which may erupt in a crowded arrangement.

What is Teething?

Teething is a phase in early childhood during which the milk teeth emerge into the mouth cutting through the gums. Children experience discomfort during this phase, and may have disturbed sleep, eating problems and may be restless and cranky.

Can Teething Cause Illnesses?

Teething is often blamed for systemic conditions like diarrhea, vomiting and fever. The possible explanation for this is that during teething the child has a tendency to chew objects for relief, which at times may not be clean and may be a source of microbes.

CHILDHOOD

When Do Permanent Teeth Appear?

The permanent teeth start erupting by about 6 years of age. Most of the permanent teeth erupt by 12 years of age except the third molars or the wisdom teeth, which erupt any time between 18 -25 years of age.

Is it Normal to Have Extra Teeth?

Sometimes children have an extra tooth or teeth. These are called supernumerary teeth, and they may appear as normal looking teeth or may be odd shaped. An example of extra teeth is a mesiodens, which may occur as a cone shaped tooth in the midline between the two upper incisors. The presence of extra teeth cannot be considered normal as they upset the normal dental balance. Thus, they may have to be extracted followed by orthodontic treatment.

Is it Normal to Have Differently Sized or Shaped Teeth?

Teeth vary slightly from person to person in their shape and size. However, it is common to find teeth that are odd shaped or sized. Some people have a few teeth that are too small: i.e. being a peg shaped tooth. Teeth that are bigger than normal can also occur. They are called Macrodont. Some of these teeth may be reshaped by the dentist to resemble normal teeth, and some may require a crown over them to make them look more normal.

What are Mammelons?

The cutting edges of the newly emerged front permanent teeth (incisors) are not even. They show elevations called mammelons that correspond to their developmental lobes. These in due course wear off to form a flat cutting edge.

What is the "Ugly Duckling" Stage?

The "Ugly Duckling" stage is a transient phase during childhood when there may be a very large space (diastema) in the middle between the two upper incisors, which can also be flaring. This occurs due to pressures from adjacent erupting teeth. This stage corrects on its own and does not require any orthodontic intervention.

How Often and How Should a Child Brush?

It is a good habit to brush the teeth both mornings, soon after getting up, and just before going to bed at night. Children should also be told to gargle every time after something is eaten. Brushing in a hurry does not help because this can mean cutting corners and making mistakes. Slow down and remove the soft sticky plaque deposit from every surface of every tooth. Harder deposits are tartar, also known as calculus, and brushing alone will not remove it. A dentist or dental hygienist can remove it, so resist brushing harder, as this can cause toothbrush damage to the teeth. Use a soft toothbrush with a small brush head (to get in hard-to-reach spots), and a pea-sized blob of toothpaste.

Very young children usually want to imitate their parents. The easiest way to persuade children to brush and rinse, is to let them watch grownups regularly and encourage them to imitate when they show an interest. Apparently, technique is not important at an early age as healthy children are not susceptible to gum disease. Children should be getting a handle on the handle of the toothbrush at an early age, and so getting used to having one in their mouth.

Parents may do some brushing for them, with lots of laughter i.e. not to make it an unpleasant experience. Gently done, it can be a bonding experience. The more comfortable and enjoyable the experience is, the less likely it is that the child will later rebel and begin to associate teeth with unpleasantness.

Later, put focus on the little ditch called the sulcus, which is situated between the tooth and the gum around each tooth. This little ditch is the place where gum disease begins. The brush is angled at a 45 degree angle to the gum (into the little ditch). The movement of the brush should be a backwards and forwards vibration or short circular movements (like a washing machine). No scrubbing is necessary.

Good Method – The Bus Route Rule

My dentist recommends the 'Bus Route Rule' i.e. use a specific direction for cleaning and stick to it. This means always starting in the same place and always finishing in the same place with the direction in between always the same – just like the bus.

"Every route takes in every surface of every tooth, and whatever route you choose you stick to it". That way you are unlikely to miss some areas while doing others twice. Especially difficult or awkward areas require a bus stop and receive extra attention.

How is Fluoridated Toothpaste Useful?

Fluorides used in toothpastes have the ability to incorporate into the tooth structure and make the teeth more resistant to dental decay. The use of fluorides may even arrest progression of caries in the initial stages.

What is Dental Decay?

Dental decay or dental caries is a disease affecting the teeth wherein they are destroyed by softening and is caused by microorganisms or germs that exist on and around the teeth. This destruction of the tooth structure occurs in the presence of the stagnated food particles.

Why Do Teeth Get Decayed?

Dental decay is the most prevalent disease affecting humanity. Teeth get decayed due to a combination of causes that include bad oral hygiene, stagnation of food on or around the teeth, presence of plaque on the tooth structure and the presence of caries causing micro-organisms.

Food particles and micro-organisms tend to stagnate in the deep pits and fissures found on the grinding surface of the teeth thereby predisposing them to dental decay. In addition, plaque and tartar may contribute to retention of particles and microbes close to the tooth structure.

How is Tooth Decay Prevented?

Prevention is always better than cure. The following factors help in prevention of caries.

- Maintenance of good oral hygiene by regular brushing and use of interdental aids (flossing/gum massage).

- Diet is a very important consideration in dental decay. Sticky food and refined sugars are important factors predisposing to caries. Thus, these foodstuffs should be avoided. Children are advised to brush immediately after they consume such foodstuffs.

- The use of fluoridated toothpaste markedly reduces the occurrence of dental decay. The dentist will advise on the use of fluoridated toothpastes.

- In some children, the grinding surface of the teeth tends to have very deep pits and grooves which predisposes them to stagnation of food and microbes. For such teeth, the dentist may use pit and fissure sealants to reduce their depth.

- Regular check-ups by the dentist to arrest caries that have just begun and for professional fluoride application.

What is Pulpotomy?

Deep inside the tooth is the dental pulp, the vital tissue that contains nerves, blood vessels and other tissues. This tissue is protected by an outer covering of dentin and enamel. When a cavity becomes large and deep, the caries may reach the inner vital tissue of the pulp, and the area of pulp adjacent to the dental decay may become infected and inflamed.

Pulpotomy is the procedure where the superficial part of the infected pulp adjacent to the area of dental decay is removed, but leaving behind the deeper pulp present inside. The procedure involves clearing all the decayed tissue and removing a part of the pulp tissue followed by treatment by some medications to promote healing of the rest of the pulp.

Is it Normal for a Child to Suck Their Finger?

It can be considered quite normal for children to suck their finger(s) up to a certain age. Continued finger sucking beyond 3 years of age may cause serious defects in the developing oral and facial structures.

Many children develop the habit of sucking the thumb or other fingers. A number of possible causes exist for finger sucking, including:

- Lack of adequate nursing or feeding.
- Feeling of insecurity due to inadequate parental care, love and affection.
- Sudden change in domestic or work atmosphere which the child cannot cope with.
- Stress related to school, friends, etc.

Finger sucking may not cause irreversible harm in children less than 3 years of age. However, much depends on factors such as duration, intensity and frequency of the sucking habit. Continuation of the habit beyond 3 years may pose problems for the developing facial and dental structures. The teeth can move forwards and an open bite can occur.

Thumb sucking can cause problems if allowed to persist beyond 3 years of age. Some of the effects include the front teeth being pushed too far forward, causing spacing of the teeth and therefore poor facial appearance. Continued indulgence in the habit may cause defects in the developing jaw and facial bones.

What About Biting Nails, a Pencil, etc., Causing Harm?

Habits like biting nails, pencils, etc. besides causing wear of the teeth can cause injury to the gums and supporting structures around the teeth.

How Does a Dentist Control Finger Sucking?

Many children stop sucking the thumb when the causative factor is identified and eliminated. Slightly older children can be reasoned out of the habit by explaining the bad effects of the habit. The dentist may sometimes advise the use of finger bandaging or the use of bitter medicine to make the habit less pleasurable. When these simple steps fail, the dentist may prescribe a "habit breaker", which is placed behind the front teeth, preventing the child from sucking the thumb.

TEENS

Dentistry for adolescents and teens

Dentistry for adolescents and teens is a fundamental part of the training the pediatric dentist receives.

Developmental Issues

Teens have all their permanent teeth except wisdom teeth (third molars) which will be developing. During these growing years, their face and jaws will undergo many changes and, although most develop normally, sometimes a tooth or teeth need to be removed due to poor position and lack of space. Regular visits are essential even though the teen may complain or think such visits a nuisance, "boring".

Dental problems can occur as tooth decay may begin to be a problem during the teen years.

Gum disease (gingivitis) is a risk. It causes red and swollen gums, bleeding gums and bad breath. The teeth and gums can stay healthy and attractive with good oral hygiene and taking good care of your teeth and diet. Gum disease may lead to anxiety or isolation issues as it affects appearance, which is so important to teens.

Dental Hygiene Guidelines for Teens

- Brush twice a day using fluoride toothpaste to remove plaque. Plaque is the main cause of tooth decay and gum disease.

- Floss daily to remove plaque from between teeth and under the gum line. If plaque is not removed daily, it can harden into tartar (unsightly, hard yellow build-up).

- Limit snacks, especially sticky, sugary or starchy foods. Prevent cavities by replacing these with bite-sized fruit and vegetables. Snacks should never take the place of nutritionally balanced meals.

- Eliminate or at least greatly reduce soda drinks and drink bottled or tap water containing fluoride which will strengthen teeth, prevent dehydration and clean excessive bacteria in mouth.

- Brush teeth for the length of one song (turn your IPod on!). Do this three times a day and proper brushing time is achieved as well as visible results.

- Wear a mouth guard for any sport or activity in which your mouth can be hit.

- Buckle up in the car. A seat belt and shoulder harness can keep your face from striking the steering wheel, the dashboard or windshield during minor accidents.

- Visit the dentist regularly for professional cleanings and checkups.

Braces

Pre-teens and teens often require braces to fix crowded or crooked teeth and poor jaw alignment. This is because teeth that do fit together incorrectly are harder to keep clean, may be lost early, and cause extra stress on the chewing muscles. Those teens who wear braces need to take extra care to clean their teeth properly.

Metal braces can scratch genital areas or rip a hole in a condom, increasing the potential for sexually transmitted diseases such as HIV/AIDS. Teens should take care during sex or long kissing sessions because the brackets can tear delicate mouth tissues and genital areas or rip a hole in a condom thereby increasing exposure to blood-borne pathogens and STDs including HIV/AIDs. Dental dams, made of latex, are advised for women for protection.

Mouth Guards

Mouth guards protect the smile of those sporty teens! They often cover upper teeth as protection against broken teeth, cut lips and other damage and they can be used to protect other fixed dental appliances (e.g. a bridge) on the lower jaw. The pressures they exert on the teeth may force them into abnormal positions which may necessitate orthodontic treatment.

What is Tongue Thrusting?

Tongue thrusting is a habit wherein the person forces the tongue against the back surface of the front teeth while swallowing. This habit can produce proclination of the front teeth and spaces between them. The dentist may have to train the patient on the correct swallowing method by some exercises and use of habit breaking devices.

What is Cleft Lip and Palate?

Clefts of the lip and palate are a very common occurrence. They are congenital deformities (defective developments) seen at the time of birth.

Cleft lip is seen as a clefting of the lip - usually the upper. This produces bad facial appearance. Cleft palate is seen as a cleft or furrow in the palate sometimes producing a communication between the nose and the mouth. This causes difficulty in nursing the child and may later pose problems of speech.

The clefts of the lip and palate occur due to a variety of reasons, the most important being genetic. The other causes include the intake of certain teratogenic drugs or chemicals during pregnancy, which cause a defect in the development.

Clefts pose numerous problems and are treated by a multidisciplinary approach that involves: the pediatrician, orthodontist, pediatric dentist, plastic surgeon, prosthodontist etc.

Nutrition

Preventative nutrition is essential to dental health as sugars and starches in snack foods and drinks sustain the development of plaque, which destroys tooth enamel. Teens need to limit the number of snacks they have because each time we consume sugars or starches, our teeth are attacked for 20 minutes or more by damaging acids.

Hypnotherapists can use their skills to ensure dental patients eat a well-balanced diet from the five food groups and for snacks, choose nutritious foods such as cheese, raw vegetables, plain yogurt or fruit. Teens can keep travel-size brushes in lockers or back packs and drink water throughout the day to help cleanse the teeth of excess bacteria and food debris as well as eat slowly with mindfulness to avoid weight gain. Chewing sugarless gum with xylitol after meals or snacks can also help cleanse the mouth.

Eating disorders

Anorexia is self-induced starvation with an inordinate fear of gaining weight, often results in vomiting, results in inadequate nutrients. This damages not only teeth but also muscles and major organs. A dentist can correct the deteriorating tooth enamel but cannot treat the sad eating disorder

Bulimia is becoming more and more common in teens. Repeated binge eating is often accompanied by self-induced vomiting, exposes teeth to strong acids that erode the tooth enamel. It is harmful to overall health and destructive to teeth as, over time, teeth exposed to stomach acids become worn, translucent and decay easily. In addition the mouth, throat and salivary glands may become swollen and tender. Bad breath is another consequence.

Both Anorexia and bulimia can respond well to hypnosis and hypnotists can work together with the client's doctor and parents.

Smoking

A hypnotist can help young teens who want and choose to follow the hypnotists instructions by giving suggestions which counteract tobacco company campaigns and peer pressure. Often they will never smoke or chew tobacco. What a great investment in the future health of a child! In addition to so many health problems, smoking stains teeth and gums. It even stains the tartar build-up on teeth and contributes to bad breath. Chewing tobacco, cigarettes and cigars increase risks of developing oral cancer and gum disease.

Smoking affects tooth growth. If a child gets to 18 years of age without smoking, it is less likely s/he will ever be tobacco dependent (Dr. Theresa Madden, faculty member at the School of Dentistry of the Oregon Health Sciences University. With Ph.D. in microbiology and immunology)

Oral Piercing

Although popular with teens oral piercing can cause complications including infections, uncontrollable bleeding, pain and nerve damage. Jewelry can chip or crack teeth causing injury to gum tissue needing prolonged healing time of a month or more.

Piercings may fracture teeth and tooth enamel which may then require fillings, root canal or even extraction. Teens have been known to choke on studs, barbells, or hoops that come loose, and the metal jewelry can also chip or crack teeth and damage their gums.

Whitening

Teens become self-conscious of their teeth, which may lead to diminished self-confidence and self-esteem issues. Using a whitening toothpaste can help remove surface stains between dental visits. Some will need to be professionally whitened to remove long-term stubborn external stains. Internal stains can be bleached, bonded or capped (crowned). Hypnotherapists can make suggestions for self-esteem in all hypnosis sessions.

2. CHILDREN AND HYPNOSIS

Children encounter many of the same types of problems as adults, plus an entire spectrum of their own. When dealing with children there are many more types of hypnotic sessions available to the consulting hypnotist than working with adults.

Children, like adults, may be helped with issues including: self-confidence, weight loss, stuttering, procrastination, improving memory, concentration, nail biting, poor sleep habits, etc....

Children may have their own list of situations that hypnosis can help them with: bed wetting, conduct at school, thumb sucking, untidiness, swearing, establishing a value system, getting along with others, loudness, insecurity, fears and nervous habits, etc.

Young children are naturally wiggly. Just because they wiggle does not mean they are not in hypnosis. Capture their imagination with a story and they get it... so let them wiggle. Just let the parents know it is normal.

RAPPORT, MIRRORING, PACING AND LEADING

Being in rapport and mirroring with children works exactly the same way as it does with adult clients. The five major areas to pace are:

- breathing
- gestures
- eye movements
- volume and tone
- vocabulary

Once we have established the correct pace, it is extremely easy to start leading them so they listen and follow instructions. Correct pacing and leading with children accomplishes the following three objectives: builds trust, creates rapport, and establishes strategies.

EVERYTHING IS A GAME

This is the time for each therapist to bring out their "inner child". Remember, each of us has been a child in the past. I read a statement that describes this nicely, *"Adults Are Simply Children Grown Tall"*. So do not be afraid to allow that child within you to emerge and relate with the child client. And use your creative mind to turn a task into a game. Once the child enjoys the behavior, he or she will duplicate the new behavior until it becomes part of their lives.

THE POWER OF IMAGINATION

Using guided imagery techniques with emotionally disturbed children has taught me a great deal about the powerful effect of this process for helping children deal with their fears, perceptions, dreams and ideas. In the process of exploring imagery and images, I have made many discoveries...not only about the process but also about children. Indeed, the children are my teachers. It is through them that I learn what works.

One of my popular props is Herbie (Hettie for the girls) the Hippo, a large velvety-soft toy. He is very gentle and the children trust that it will carry them safely through any adventure. He lives in Africa where there are no dentists, so I have the children "reverse nag" i.e. tell Herbie the advantages of going to the dentist and how s/he's a good guy. If they do not, they will tell Herbie their fears and when we listen carefully we get cues to help us when making suggestions, talking to parts or regressing to cause.

I use other props too-- balloons, bubbles, streamers-- anything that will activate the imagination, and help the children to move from the concrete to the abstract, for they are still very concrete in their conceptualizing.

Another discovery I made is that some of the children are not ready for kinesthetic imagery, internalized movement control. They try to lie quietly, visualizing as we take our journeys, but I see their muscles twitching, and know they still need to be actively involved. So, as a preliminary to guided imagery, we often do creative movement imagery, directly moving to the imagery story, thus allowing kinesthetic integration. The children who need to actively participate, are not quite developmentally ready for the internalized movement control, but guided imagery can be an aid to transition from one stage to the next. Sometimes I offer active movement imaging, followed by a related internalized guided imagery experience.

Although my guided imagery adventures are varied and eclectic, when done in a group the bedtime routine is personalized and individual. The bedtime imagery serves several purposes. It helps the kids let go of the anxiety, fear and anger built up over the day. It helps them let go of the struggles in daily living and it helps them to relax so they can sleep comfortably without night terrors and nightmares.

LET YOUR INNER CHILD EMERGE

The dentist can distract children with intense imagery. For example: one dentist describes how he is removing the bugs that have been clinging on to the child's teeth. He even has the child draw them with colors in the waiting room beforehand so he (the dentist will know what to look for!   As the dentist is working he says thing such as: *"Well we've got rid of most of those Klingon Bugs now. Now, I'm going to swap to a different cleaner to get rid of the last few bugs…. this one will wobble your tooth a bit…. can you feel how I am chasing those naughty Klingon Bugs…. I'm chasing them round and round and round your tooth…. I'm really tickling them and they are laughing and falling off you tooth … can you feel me tickling them?"*

For sensations experienced during an extraction

This was my first personal experience of dentistry. I cannot recall anything about the experience other than the feeling of pressure. I cannot recall the injections, tastes or smells, just the feeling of a large amount of force being applied to my upper jaw.

"OK Jo, I've made your tooth really numb. Now in a moment I'm going to start wiggling it out. You are going to feel me pushing, you will feel lots of PRESSURE, you will feel it wiggling but it WILL NOT bother you because I've made it so numb."

3. SCRIPTS FOR WORKING WITH CHILDREN

Scripts are found under heading indicators:

> **Inductions (A)**
>
> **Deepeners (B)**
>
> **Suggestions and Reinforcers (C)**
>
> **Emerging (D)**

MAGIC TV INDUCTION (Ages 3 to 9 years) (A)

Would you like to watch my TV? (As soon as child nods agreement say) *Close your eyes and make yourself as limber (loose) as a rag doll… That's fine. Now let's make believe we are going to your house.*

You walk up the walk, open the door and walk into the room where the TV is. I'll turn on the set as you lie down on the floor and get ready to look at the picture. First, we can hear the sound. Now, here comes the picture. … The cartoons are on and all your favorite cartoon characters are mixed up together. How many different cartoon characters are there? Which one do you like the best?

If you open your eyes, the cartoon characters will go away. As you look up at the cartoons, isn't it funny, you can't open your eyes. You don't want to open your eyes because you want to watch the cartoon show, and you continue to watch the show, because you find it so easy to watch with your eyes closed

Now, you continue watching this cartoon show and you don't have to pay any attention to me unless I tap you on the shoulder like this. (press shoulder) I will be talking to you, but you won't pay any attention to me unless I press your shoulder. Now just watch this funny cartoon show because the longer you watch it, the funnier it gets and the more relaxed you become. (Begin suggestions)

BUCKET OF WATER INDUCTION (Ages 5 to 10) (A)

(Have the child sit in a very comfortable position and ask him/her if they would like to play a game of imagination. When the child says yes, say;)

Now just close your eyes and keep them closed until I ask you to open them. I want you to imagine or just pretend that, on the floor of the right side of your chair, is a large bucket of warm water. It is easily in reach with your right hand. *(Establish that the child knows left from right, if not, indicate which hand by touching the appropriate hand.)*

I want you to imagine or just pretend that floating on top of the water in the bucket is a large rubber ball. What color is the ball?... *(Have child indicate the color of ball.)* Now put your hand on top of the ball and push the ball down to the bottom of the bucket.

Now release the ball and notice how it floats right back up to the surface. Now, I want you to keep pressing the ball up and down in the bucket. Notice that each time you press the ball down into the bucket you grow more and more relaxed...More and more sleepy...

That's right!. Just keep pushing the rubber ball up and down in the bucket and notice how you are growing sleepier and sleepier. No matter how sleepy you become, you will always be able to hear my voice and the sound of my voice will help you to relax even more. ...That's right... just keep pressing that (color) ball up and down and notice how you can sleep deeper and deeper.

(At this point you may either do a 5 down to one deepening technique or allow the child to continue deepening his own trance and begin the programming portion of the session.)

FACE ON THUMB INDUCTION (Ages 5 to 10) (A)

Ask the child if he/she wants to play a neat came. When the child says yes, on the child's thumb closest to you draw a picture of a happy face. (Put happy face on the thumb so it shows when palms of hands facing downward.) Then place his/her hand on his/her lap with the palms facing down. Tell the child to fix his/her gaze on the thumb and not to take his/her eyes off of it.

Next, place your hand over the child's hand being careful not to cover the happy face. Start to exert a gentle pressure down on the hand while at the same time giving the suggestion that his hand is becoming heavier and heavier.

Gradually lift the pressure off the hand and as the pressure slackens, tell the child that his/her hand feels light and airy and floats gently upward into the air, towards his/her face. Have the child continue to watch the face on his/her thumb as it comes closer and closer to his/her face.

(When the hand touches his/her face, he/she is told his/her) eyes will close and he/she will go deeply to sleep. Be sure to tell the child that he/she will be able to hear everything that is said.

"As your eyes close, your hand descends or falls slowly to your lap and you feel relaxed all over and become soft and limb as a rag doll.

After the child is in hypnosis, tell him/her to slowly, but silently begin to count backwards from 100 to zero. Tell the child that as he/she is doing this he/she will continue to hear your voice, but not to pay any attention to it. Tell him that when he reaches zero to raise a finger on the hand closest to you to let you know that he is finished.

NUMB HAND (C)

Induction of choice …. Check for somnambulism … followed by…..

… I'm going to put some ointment on your hand that will make it feel numb. [*Note: If you actually have a topical anesthetic available, or if a physician is in attendance and can apply such an anesthetic, so much the better. If not rubbing alcohol, or some other cooling substance with color or fragrance, will suffice.*]

I know it smells a little funny, but it will make your hand grow numb in a very short amount of time. Then, when your hand is numb, you can put it on any part of your body and let the numbness go from your hand into the part that hurts.

Now, I don't know if your hand will become completely numb or not… it may just will feel like you are wearing a thin rubber glove, like the kind doctors get to wear... *(Pause up to one minute)*

Okay, I think it's ready. *(Grasp-child by the wrist. Too much touching of the hand over stimulates it and ruins the effect.)*

Let's lay your hand on <u>(name the body part)</u>, and then just relax and imagine how the numbness is going into the part that hurts. *(Pause.)*

And, the hurt gets smaller and smaller. By the way, can you think of a color that the numbness might be? I mean, if we were just pretending it really was a color. Can you think of a color that might go with the numbness? *(Wait for response.)* Great, now just imagine that color going from you

REGRESSION WITH CHILDREN

Anything that you have ever seen, anything that you have ever heard, anything that you have ever felt before in your life is stored within your own magic mind, yes, and that is why we call it your magic mind – your subconscious. That's right! Anything that we have stored in our own minds, we can bring back. Now, I'm going to count from three down to one. As I count back, you are going to actually get to travel back in time.

[99]

You are going to get to travel all the way back in time to the age of five. You will be five years old again.

Three ... feel yourself as you are becoming younger and smaller, getting younger and smaller going back, back to age five.

Two ... That's right. All the way back to five years old. There you are. ...Almost there. Get ready. And...

One ... you're back--five years old. Five years old and happy. As soon as you are back to five years old, I want to speak to five.

When you are there just raise your yes finger to let me know. Good.

Now, you're five years old and five is different from the age you were before. Even with your eyes closed still, I want you to look down at your feet and tell me what you are wearing on your feet now that you are five years old.

That's good. Now tell me what else you are wearing. Five years old. Tell me five – do you ever (suck your blanket, grind your teeth, gag on your toothbrush etc.)

MAGIC STORY INDUCTION FOR CHILDREN (Ages 6 to 10)

Lie back now, and you can close your eyes and feel really safe as I take hold of your hand, because I will tell you a magic story. You like magic stories, don't you? ... It is a story about a very special place, deep in an enchanted forest, where everything I tell you will come true. ... It is a magic story because, if you hold on to my hand and believe hard enough, it will really take as there. ... So listen carefully and hold on to my hand, and soon we will be deep in the magic, special place where everything I tell you will come true.

Imagine now that we are walking together down a long winding path which runs through the middle of a large patch of woods. ... We are walking along hand in hand, early on a bright spring morning. ... Birds are singing in the trees, and here and there a flower is poking its head out of the soft, green grass which grows beside the path. ... And because this is a magic story, the further we go along the path the more real everything becomes. ...

Now and then, a ray of sunlight makes its way down through the branches of the trees and falls upon the dewdrops in the grass, causing them to sparkle like a million tiny diamonds ... The air is fresh and cool, with gentle breezes blowing now and then. Blowing out and then, causing the trees. the grass and the flowers to move ever so slightly, as if everything in the world were feeling so happy on this bright spring morning... that nothing was able to keep still for long... And, because this is a magic story, the further we go along the path, the more real everything becomes.

As we continue on our walk, we can begin to be aware of the sound of rushing water... With each second, the sound becomes clearer and clearer still... And now, we are standing beside the bank of a forest stream, which is making the sound we have been hearing...

The water is flowing past us swiftly and clearly, for it has come tumbling down from a magic spring many miles away in the hills... And because the water from the magic spring is enchanted, anyone who drinks it will be enchanted to... And s/he will easily be able to find that special place in the forest where everything I tell him/her will come true...

We dip our hands eagerly into the bubbling stream, and cup them together, bringing the cool fresh water to our lips again and again, until we have taken all we want...

Now it is time to hurry on our way once more; for the water from the magic spring has made it certain that we will soon find that very special place in the enchanted forest, where everything I say will come true; and we know now that it cannot be far away...

As we continue on our journey, we notice a tiny path leading off to one side, and we decide to go up this path in order to see where it leads... Before very long, we notice that the woods are beginning to thin out, and that we are about to enter a clearing... And as we approach nearer and nearer to the edge of the clearing, we can see that the path we have been following leads up to a small cottage...

This is that very special place I have been telling you about, where everything I say will really happen... The door to the cottage is slightly open as we hurry up the path, and as soon as we reach the entrance we hurry on inside in order to lose no more time. In order to lose no more time... We have arrived now, at that enchanting, magical place in the enchanted forest which we have traveled so far to reach.. And as long as we remain here, in this enchanting place everything I say and everything I describe to you will come true as soon as I have said it.

(Here is where you make suggestions for things that have happened in the past no longer bothering him/her and imagery for future visits to the dentist being just another thing to do, no longer bothering the child)

In just a moment we are going to leave the enchanted cottage, and go back down the path and through the woods to the world outside. But the things that I have told you while we were here in the magic cottage will continue to be true even after we return, and we will be able to come back to this special place whenever I tell the magic story that takes us there... Now we are going out of the door and starting back along the path... but everything I have told you will still be true, after we return...

Now we are coming out of the woods, and hurrying back along the park that brought us here. Now we are coming back to the first path, which

runs along the side of the enchanted stream from which we drank...
Soon we will be back in the world outside, feeling rested and because of
all the wonderful things that happened to us while we were here...

Now we are passing by the enchanted stream, and soon we will be out
of the forest and you will be able to open your eyes, feeling wonderful.
And all that I told you will still be true...You can open your eyes now,
feeling wonderful. *(Emerge)*

ELIMINATE SUGARS (C)

We have learned that the way to look after your teeth and make them
strong so you can eliminate having more and more teeth falling out
before they should and more and more dentist visits, is to stop eating
all of those sugary types of food. You will need to help me because you
know what the sugary sweet foods are. You know the ones that you
need to get rid of, isn't that right? Earlier you told me what they were.
Let me see if I can remember. Cakes, cookies, ice cream, sodas, pies,
and candies. I think that is most of them. We know that these kinds of
foods are just full of sugar. In the past you thought a lot about these
kinds of food. Today if you are thinking about these kinds of foods you
are going to be thinking about how sugary, sicky and kind of sticky they
are.

You wouldn't want to eat a bowl of cereal with a hundred pounds of
sugar on top would you? Well that's what it's like when you eat sugary
things. You no longer want to eat cakes, cookies, candies, ice cream,
soda and pies because they are filled with sugar.

You're a smart kid. And like all smart kids you know how to work a
television set isn't that right? We might be watching something and
when we don't like it, what do we do? We change the channels. Yes,
you are right. You are going to do the same thing about the sugars. You
are going to change the channels in your own mind. You are going to
change your mind. You have a right to change your mind on those
things now. You used to wear diapers, but you don't any more. You
used to sit in a baby high chair, you don't do that now. You used to eat
sugary food... you no longer do that now and you LOVE to say NO to
sugary foods, it's fun to say NO instead of saying yes, isn't it? Now. You
are allowed to say NO as much as you like to sugary foods and snacks
around you. Let's practice that now....

THUMB SUCKING (C)

You have decided that the time has come to stop sucking your thumb
and grow strong adult teeth. You are doing this because you know it is
the right thing for you to do. In the past when you were smaller, sucking

your thumb seemed like the right thing to do, but now that you are older, the idea of sucking your thumb has become kind of silly. It seems like a silly thing to do. It would seem silly to sit around and suck on our toes wouldn't it? It would seem silly to try to suck on our elbow, isn't that right? Of course it would be awfully hard to try to suck on your ears. Of course, it really seems kind of silly to be sucking on your thumb.

From this moment on, if you have the thought or idea of sucking on your thumb, you are going to take in a real deep breath and just hold it for about two or three seconds. One, two, three, let it out and you will find that the thought, the idea of sucking your thumb, will just disappear. What you are now doing is sucking in air. Air is good. We need air. We don't need to suck thumbs. Everytime, if you have a thought or idea of sucking your thumb, you will take in a deep breath, hold it for one, two, three, and let it out. Everytime, if the old thought of sucking your thumb would pop into your mind, you know what to do. Isn't that right? There's always something better to do than suck on your thumb – I wonder what you'll be doing now....

NAIL BITING (C)

You are going to be very happy to realize that you have already stopped biting your nails. That's right. You will realize how good you will feel right now even though you are not chewing or biting or picking at your nails. This nice, good feeling that you are experiencing right now is a feeling that you made happen. No one else may ever make you relax just as no one else can ever make you bite your nails. You are in control. You are the boss.

You have control over the movements of your hands and your arms. If you wanted to choose, if you decided to, you could move your hands and place them on your legs. If you wanted to, if you decided to, you could move your hands and place them on your tummy. If you wanted to, if you needed to, you could move your hands and place them right on the top of your head. Yes, you have control over the movements of your hands. If your hands or arms would ever begin to sneak up towards your mouth for the purpose of biting or chewing on your nails, you will become aware of it and you will then move your hands to another place or position. They can never ever move up towards your mouth without you noticing it.

Once you notice that they are sneaking up towards your mouth for the purpose of biting or chewing on your nails, you'll move your hands away and feel real good. As you continue to relax let one of your hands try to sneak up toward your mouth and notice how you catch it. When you catch that hand moving up towards your mouth, move it away. Bring it back down to the arm of the chair.

Let's see if it is going to be your right hand or your left hand that is going to try to sneak up without you knowing it. There they go. As soon as you know that it is moving up towards your mouth, you catch it and move it back down to the arm of the chair. That was good. So if those hands and arms try to sneak up towards your mouth for the purpose of biting your nails you will know it and you will move it to some other position.

STRESS (C)

I want you to realize that you have the ability to feel either relaxed or to feel really tense. To demonstrate this I am going to come over and touch your right arm. As I touch your right arm, let every muscle, every tendon, and every ligament in your arm feels lose and limp. Feel it now. Lose, limp and relaxed and at ease like an old rag doll. I'm lifting it up. When I let go of it, it just flops right back down to the arm of the chair. Now that is what we call being relaxed. I am going to come over and touch your left arm. As I touch your left arm, I am extending it straight out in front of you. As I touch your left arm, feel the muscles becoming tight and rigid.

In fact, the left hand and arm is feeling tight and so rigid it is beginning to feel as though the left hand and arm is stiff as a steel beam. Stiff as a steel beam, so stiff, so rigid that it won't even bend anymore. I want you to go ahead and try. Attempt to bend it. It is so stiff, so tense that it just won't bend. Try to bend it. It just will not bend. Now that is total stress. Tightness! There is only one person in the world that can make you relax. That person is you. That's right. You have the ability to relax.

I am going to give you the words that will allow you to relax whenever you want, wherever you might be. I want you now to say the words to yourself, "Relax now". As you say the words "relax now" to yourself notice that the tension, the tightness in that left arm just disappears and you can bend the arm, it flops back to the arm of the chair. Say the words "relax now" to yourself. Anytime you say the words "relax now", you will be relaxed. This will be your secret words that will work forever.

FEAR #1 (C) (Thunderstorms or other fears)

In just a moment, I am going to come over and touch your right hand. As I touch your right hand, you are going to feel one of the happiest feelings of your life. It might have been a time when you won a contest, or received a special gift. It will be a very happy time for you. As I touch your right hand now, you are beginning to remember and create those happy feelings again. As you start to feel those happy feelings, I would like you to nod your head yes. Good, now each time I touch your right hand, feel those happy feelings again. Each time I touch your hand the feelings become stronger.

I am now going to touch your left hand. As I touch your left hand I want you to remember the last time you had a fear of storms - when you felt afraid of that storm *(or whatever the fear is)*. As I touch your left hand I want you now to bring back some of those fears of storms again.

Think about storms. Feel some of the feelings about storms as I touch your left hand.

You are beginning to feel those feelings, kind of scared, kind of frightened. As you begin to feel those feeling of being afraid of thunderstorms, I want you to shake your head yes. Good. Each time I touch your hand feel the feelings getting stronger. Touch your hand again, that left hand; feelings become stronger. Now I want you to think about a thunderstorm as I touch your left hand. I know that is kind of frightening, isn't it? Now watch what happens...

FEAR #2 (C)   (Fear of Dogs)

I am going to count from three down to one. As I count back you are going to begin to see a movie. It is going to be a movie about the time you first started to be afraid of dogs *(or whatever the fear is)*. You won't be afraid but you will remember the first time that you had that fear.

Three. Two. One. You are beginning to remember. There it is, like watching a movie, that first time you had a fear of dogs. As that movie becomes clearer, as you begin to remember that, I want you to shake your head yes. Now as I touch your right hand, I want you to tell me what is happening and how old you are. OK. You were four years old and a dog bit you. That was frightening, wasn't it? Yes. Of course it was. Now has a dog ever bit you since? No. So, it makes sense to be afraid of dogs when they bite you, but there is no need to be afraid of dogs if they don't bite you. I am going to count from three to one again and this time you are going to see a movie about a time in your life not far away when you are not afraid of dogs. Three. Two. One.

There it is, a movie of yourself, and you are not afraid of dogs anymore. Isn't that a nice movie? Yes and tell me ... How old are you in this movie? Oh, you are at the age you are now. You are not afraid of dogs anymore, are you? So, it was OK to be afraid when you were four because you were just a little kid. But, now, being nine, you don't have to be afraid. When we finish today you won't be afraid of dogs anymore because the movie you are seeing is becoming real. So, I want you to think about yourself. You are out playing and there is a friendly dog around but now you are not afraid, are you? No. I want you to think that you went to someone's house with your mom and dad and they had a dog. But, now you are not afraid, are you? No. You won't ever be afraid again, will you? No, I didn't think so.

FEAR #3 (C)

Now with your eyes closed I want you to think about the bravest person in the whole world. It might be someone one real. It might be someone imaginary. It might be a cartoon, but with someone that you think is the bravest person in the whole world, and as you begin to know who the bravest person in the whole world is. I want you to shake your head yes. Good.

Now I am going to touch your right hand, and as I touch your right hand I want you to tell me who that person is. I'm touching your right hand and who is that bravest person in the whole world? "It's Batman." Oh, Batman is pretty brave. Batman is probably not afraid of anything is he? No and if you were Batman's friend, if he could be with you, you wouldn't be afraid either would you? No. Let's see, pretend you could talk to Batman and he is pretty smart not only brave but he is smart.

Ask Batman if he likes you. What did he say? He does. I thought he did. Ask Batman who protects people and who's a good guy if he would be willing to be your friend and protect you? What did he say? He would, that's great. Because from now on if you would ever start to become afraid, all you have to do is close your eyes for a second and you will be able to see Batman just like you can now. Can you see him? Yes, and you will know that he is right there with you and he won't let anything happen to you.

Now I want you to think about something that used to cause you to have fear. Close your eyes even tighter and there is Batman, and you're not afraid anymore are you? No. Because Batman is there for you, and he will be with your forever, because we know Batman will always do the right thing. So he will protect you and as long as Batman is your friend, and he is going to be your friend forever, you won't ever be afraid again will you? No, I didn't think so. That's good.

You and I are going to do something really magical. It might even surprise you. Now, I want you to pretend that there was a light switch on the wall and if we flipped this switch, what happens? It doesn't turn on a light; it doesn't turn off a light. What it does is it turns off all the feeling in your right hand so you can't feel any pain. You can't feel anything in your hand.

So, now reach up with your left hand, reach high up into the air. There you go ... start to flip that switch, pull it down, pull it down, pull it down until it's all the way off and you have turned off any pain in your hand, and once you have flipped the switch all the way and all the pain is gone, I want you to shake your head yes, so you can't feel anything in your right hand. That's good. That's good. Now, I'm going to lift up your right hand. It just feels good and you can hardly feel that hand at all can you? No. Now, in a moment, you're going to stay in this special sleep even with your eyes open.

When I ask you to close your eyes you will be able to close them and go even deeper into this sleep. I want you to go ahead and open your eyes for a moment. Look at your hand. Look how hard I have been pinching it, but you can't feel anything can you? Why can't you feel anything in that hand? That's right because you flipped the switch. Good, now I want you to close your eyes again, that's good. I'm going to put your hand back down to the arm of the chair and I want you to turn the switch back on so you can feel things in your hand. That's it; turn it back on so all the feelings are back once you have flipped the switch back on.

I want you to shake your head yes for me. Good, now the next time that you go to the doctor and he is going to give you a shot, what you are going to do is tell him to wait a minute. Just close your eyes down and you will see that switch and you will flip it down and what you are going to do is turn off all pain, all feeling for a shot and it won't bother you at all. Then when he is done you will close your eyes again and turn the switch back on. You can do that can't you?

EMERGE - POST HYPNOSIS #1 (D)

We have had a real good time today. When I bring you out of this wonderful, magical kind of sleep, you're going to feel great. When you walk back out front where your mom is waiting for you, the first thing that you are going to do is give her a big hug and a kiss. Tell her thanks for bringing you here, because you know you are going to do better. If you understand this just shake your head, yes. Good.

I am going to count from five down to one (or 1-5) and at the count of one, you will open your eyes and be wide awake. When you walk out front you will give your mom a big hug and kiss. Tell her thanks for bringing you here because you're going to do better. Five, now we have really had fun today and four some of the feeling is coming back in to those feet, those legs, hands and arms, there it is.

Three, breathing a little heavier, a little easier now you've got it. Two, coming all the way back and feeling happy, getting ready to go out and give your mom a big hug and kiss and tell her thanks for bringing you here. One, open your eyes all the way, wide awake, what a nice feeling. Let's go out front.

HOMEWORK - KEY WORD(S)

A key word is any word that the child will verbally say to reinforce a certain behavior. It is advisable to reinforce the use of the key word after the session has been completed.

The following is an example of a key word that will help a child slow-down in their speaking:

I am going to tell you a couple of magic words. These words are "slow time". Anytime you find yourself doing things or speaking rapidly, I want you to say the words, "slow time" to yourself. As you say "slow time" to yourself you will begin to relax, do things more thoughtfully, and talk more slowly. These wonderful, magic words will work for you from this moment on. You will remember the words, "slow time".

HOMEWORK - LOG BOOKS & CHARTS

Most children are looking for confirmation that they are doing well. The use of log books and or charts has been proven to be a very positive way of reinforcing the positive steps that the child has made.

In many schools the use of charts with stars has been a common practice for many years.

For the best results, it is important that the child be involved with designing and keeping up with the chart of the log book. More often than not, the parent is looking for an outstanding reward for completion of a total project where in reality a small reward such as a star or a check mark on a routine basis will usually produce the desired results.

The therapist can also implement the chart system and discuss it with the child after the session is completed.

Section 5

CASE HISTORIES

Please note that in order to keep confidentiality the names of clients have been changed and countries or residence omitted unless written permission has been given to print such details.

Case History 1: Adult Root Canal and Regression to Cause

Simone Verbiesen, 36 years old, Tilburg, The Netherlands. Simone has given her written approval that her name can be used in this text. The hypnotherapist, Ina, had an emergency call and session with a client with extreme fear of dentists, and a root canal treatment due the following Thursday. In previous dental visits, Simone feared drilling and her eyes suffered from the local anesthesia. In addition, she had a gagging problem. Previous root canal treatment had brought about such an intense fear that she was unable to keep her bowel movements controlled. Consequently, it seemed to her impossible to honor her upcoming appointment.

When there is a case of extreme fear, it is important to find the cause of the fear and give the client a new perspective with regards to the cause. So in this case, **regression to the cause** of the fear seemed important to do. This process is making use of this fear and allowing the subconscious to discover where it started and realize they survived. In this case, we used "Affect Bridge" and followed moments of fear going from 35 years back to a situation where she was 5 years old.

The first regression on her fear brought her to a situation where she was 35 years old, gagging, while the dentist was drilling a tooth. Next, she relived a situation where she was 34 years old and the dentist was giving her a root canal treatment. Next moment revealed her at the age of 16 where the dentist was angry with her because she did not brush her teeth very well. Going back further in time, we found out that at the age of 13, the dentist was drilling a tooth and she was gagging. One of the more difficult memories was at the age of 7 when she had a toothache. She was very scared and not co-operating with the dentist, who got so angry that he slapped her in the face.

These were all SSE situations (Subsequent Sensitizing Events) that were linked with dental visits. However, the surprise came in the last phase of this regression, ISE (Initial Sensitizing Event). There was still one more situation linked with this extreme fear. This last situation revealed that at the age of 5 years she had to leave her home and family to live in a children's home because her father and mother were unable to take care of her due to some physical problems. She was very scared.

What we needed to find out was how the fear of the dentist and the fear of leaving home were connected. It turned out that the underlying fear was the fact that with all these experiences, she was unable to control the situation(s).

Correcting this fear: In order to address this fear, we had Simone relive the situation from a new perspective. *'Had I only known then what I know now'.* Basically this means that the client, while in hypnosis, relives the events again from a new perception, strengthened through inner child work (a technique that basically is about being empowered with self-esteem). After that, Ina taught her to use self-hypnosis with the dentist, giving her self-control.

Results: Five days later Simone went to the dentist and was able to follow procedures without problems and without pain. She gave Ina the following testimonial in 2009 (translated)

"I cannot tell often enough what you did for me. I have had several treatments now with the dentist and periodontist, and can only say that during the root canal treatments I was in an altered state of mind. The treatment could go ahead without the anesthetic. I was very calm and I could control myself completely.

The fear I had is almost gone, except from the normal anxiety having to go to the dentist. But, I am no longer afraid. The last treatment was 2 weeks ago and I was in another state of mind, very relaxed. The treatment was over before I could even notice. It means a lot that I can apply self-hypnosis with the dentist because of the help you gave me. I cannot thank you enough for that.

I recommend your sessions to the dentist and to other people as well. Seeing the difference in me before the session and after the session, I can advise this to everybody, it means a lot."

Testimonial March 2011 (translated)

"A couple of weeks ago I went for two new crowns. Also, this time I went quietly with the idea that I have a 100% control. The dentist knows that I practice self-hypnosis and he knows what to do. At my request he tells me what he is going to do up front and that gives me peace of mind. Because I know what I can do myself, I feel so much better. I still am very thankful that you helped me on such short notice."

CASE HISTORY 2: Adult Dental Implant Surgery

50 year old Deborah was about to go through dental implant surgery with a bone graft. The surgery is usually 90 minutes long. Deborah decided to use hypnosis combined with local anesthesia instead of using IV sedation. She was fearful of not being in control with IV sedation along with her concerns of added monetary cost.

"She came to my office two weeks before the procedure to train for her hypnosis conscious sedation. She was first instructed about how we can train ourselves to get so involved in taking ourselves to a safe place- real or imagined- that we actually feel as if it is real. Almost like being dissociated from the surgery itself. She decided to use the dentist's surgery light as if it was the sun and she would be on a beach in Hawaii.

I instructed Deborah to use all of her senses. See what she would see, hear what she would hear, feel what she would feel, smell what she would smell and even taste what she would taste. We practiced this in the office as well as instructing her about how to get into self-hypnosis at home. She practiced this at home for two weeks prior to the procedure by sitting in front of a bright light.

She was instructed that upon sitting in the dental chair, the moment the dentist would shine the light on her, instantly, she would be transported to Hawaii. She even took an iPod with Hawaiian music to the dental surgery.

Result: Deborah recalls being absolutely involved in the Hawaiian scene and the music so that she did not even realize the surgery was taking a long time. The surgery had some complications so that it lasted 2 1/2 hours instead of 90 minutes. The local anesthesia started to wear off towards the end of the procedure so she really had to focus on the Hawaii scene a little more. She was aware of the pressure of the suturing but was not feeling any real pain and reported that it was the weirdest thing. The dentist reported that Deborah was more sedated than his chemically sedated patients. He was very impressed".

CASE HISTORY 3: Gag Reflex Suppression for Impressions

Sam is an 11 year old who required braces and had not been able to sit still in order for plaster impressions to be made of his teeth. He fidgeted, getting more scared with each attempt. He started gagging and panicking and the dentist was unable to get a decent impression. His mother brought him to me to help ease his anxiety which would enable getting the impressions done.

"Sam came to the office to practice going into hypnosis. During trance, a spoon was put on the tip of his tongue so that he could stay relaxed without reacting to the spoon. As the trance practice session progressed, the spoon was placed further and further back on the tongue with Sam staying relaxed without gagging. He practiced counting the number of breaths while breathing through only his nose. With each number, he felt himself in more control.

During trance, he also practiced going into trance after he sits in the dentist's chair. How did I do this? During trance, he was told to open his eyes and stand up and then sit down. When he sits down, he closes his eyes, goes more and more in control and relaxes even more. Sam enjoyed the idea that he was able to be in total control.

Result: His mother reported that he felt really "cool" about the ability to count his breaths and be in charge of how he reacted. The office staff cheered when the impressions came out of his mouth in perfect form".

CASE HISTORY 4: Young Girl with Orthodontic Palate Expander on Roof of Mouth

Ann R. is a young girl of 10 years old who needed an orthodontic appliance, called a Palate Expander, to be situated on the roof of her mouth. In the top of the appliance, there is a little hole, into which a little key fits. Each time the swivel key is inserted into the hole in the screw, and turned until the key touches the housing it is considered "one turn". There is a long string attached to the key so that when the point of the key fits into the little hole of the appliance the mother turns the key to "expand" the devise. For each full revolution of the screw, one mm of expansion is achieved.

"It was very scary for both the child and mother because the key can drop unto the back of the throat. It was uncomfortable physically as well as emotionally for the child. She had a hard time staying still as well as opening up her mouth to allow the mother to see the little hole.

Ann came into the office and we practiced going into trance and taking her to a safe place. She liked reading books, so she took herself to a scene from a Harry Potter book. We had her open up her mouth really, really wide and then just relax even more. She was instructed that the key is like a magic wand that creates her staying very relaxed and still with her mouth opened until the magic words..."O.K. It's done".

Result: Her mom called and reported "success" and was VERY happy and relaxed herself".

CASE HISTORY 5: Eleven Year Old Boy Sucking at Night and Fear of Braces

Background: Tony (not his real name) was 11 years old (five years ago) when he was referred for sucking at night. It did not matter what he sucked: sheets, T-shirt, pillow etc., his teeth were being pulled out of shape and braces were being considered. The thought of braces scared him. He did not like going to the dentist and had started intermittent gagging with cleaning his teeth. His parents found him withdrawn and isolated at home. Mum and dad both worked from home, with dad travelling out of town frequently during the week. Tony was bright, doing well in school and he loved being popular at school, where he was the class clown. He loved the beach and water sports.

First consultation: I found Tony to be an "itchity, fidgety kid" who wanted to talk a lot and ask a lot of questions (although evasive about himself). I explained my work as "working with kids' magic mind; the part that wants to be really great and do lots of good things and stop doing things they don't want to do so they could grow up to have their two minds agreeing". We made a list of things he would like to have his "magic mind" do for him.

I helped him to change his negative beliefs such as "I don't want to have braces" to "I want to grow healthy happy teeth" and I don't want my brother to keep stealing my things" to "I want my brother's behavior to no longer affect me so he no longer controls me". We did some Emotional Freedom Technique (EFT) on those feelings and he relaxed and found it fun. Then I did some suggestibility tests: hand levitation (balloon vs heavy books) and stiff arm to show how his magic mind works.

I asked him, "If there was a fear in not having something to suck on at night, what might it be?" He looked away, changed the subject and found something to play with and ask questions about. He gave permission for me to talk with his "magic mind" so we did the Bucket of Water Induction. He kept one eye on me, occasionally opening one eye to see what I was doing. However, he went into somnambulism which I tested by a hand pinch. I followed with a few suggestions about how he would feel more and more relaxed at school and even more at home, how he was loved and although only ten, he could be in control of his reactions to people, situations and events, by being in control of his reactions to those things. Time was running out so I left it there and he was very happy saying he loved the floppy feeling in his arms and shoulders and when mum asked if he would like to come again, he said "Yes".

Second consultation: As I knew we had a child with compliance, I was looking forward to getting straight into some hypnosis on the second session. Mum reported he was very keen to see me again, and Tony said he had been doing the stiff arm test on his friends and wanted to do it better. So we spent a little time on that before I asked "would you like to have that nice heavy feeling and talking to your magic mind again?" Following the Bucket of Water Induction (see scripts) I deepened him by losing numbers on the beach (writing numbers in the sand and erasing them or having the water wash them away). I had Tony imagine being in bed, asleep and feeling the need to suck. From there, I regressed Tony to the first time he had the feeling. He was five years old and not happy because he was going to school but his baby brother got to stay home. "It wasn't fair!" When I asked, was this the first time he had this feeling, he answered "no".

I told him to go back to the first time and he was three years old in his cot and listening to mum and dad arguing. Mum was saying they would have to put Tony in another room now that a new baby was on the way, Dad was upset because the other room was his office; he was saying "It's not fair" and so was mum. He was not sure who said, "There's no room for Tony" and "He will make too much noise", or if he had decided that's what they meant. He was terrified and wanted to cry but was scared of being heard and not being wanted, so he sucked on his pillow and they did not notice and he went to sleep. He said it was the first time he had this feeling.

Next morning he went to school and the teacher was so nice, she said he was special and gave him a star for his work. He loved the attention and "knew" that if he were popular, here he would be safe, so he made everyone laugh while at home he was quiet. He hated when his brother was noisy because he (Tony) was afraid he may be thrown out for causing the noise. Now when he felt those same feelings he would suck whatever cloth was closest. He was scared "because school isn't open at night".

I had him come back to the present day, in a bigger house, sharing his room with his brother, his mum and dad happy with their big home office and so much space even the TV has its own room! I had Tony feel the safety of his parent's love as ten year old Tony. I then had him go back to talk to three year old Tony, where he could surround his younger self with so much love and tell him (3 year old Tony) what 10 year old Tony knows now yet did not know then. They "spoke" to each other until younger Tony understood, and then younger Tony could understand and forgive Mum and Dad because he understood that he was not the problem.

We progressed to seven year old Tony hearing about the new baby and reassured him everything would be okay, so he forgave his parents and baby brother who wasn't even born yet (which made Tony laugh). We travelled through all the years from five through ten asking if he could sleep without the sucking now. He said yes. He said his real problem was his brother getting all the attention and him having to be quiet, so now he understood that he would give his brother attention, because that is what he secretly wanted all anyway.

I deepened Tony's trance and did some direct suggestion along the lines of:

"You have decided that the time has come to stop sucking at night. You are doing this because you know it is the right thing for you to do. In the past when you were smaller, sucking seemed like the right thing to do, but now that you are older, the idea of sucking has become kind of silly to you, for you are loved and feel great.

It would seem silly to sit around and suck on our toes wouldn't it. . . It would seem silly to try to suck on our elbow ...Of course it would be awfully hard to try to suck on your ears. It really seems kind of silly to be sucking on your sheets, pillows or blanket. From this moment on, if you have the thought or idea of sucking at night, then your magic mind will take in a real deep breath and just hold it for about two or three seconds. One, two, three, let it out and you will find that the thought, the idea of sucking anything when you are asleep is silly. You feel safe and you let the sleep come quietly and the need to suck will just disappear, no matter what is going on around you.

What you do now is to breathe, sucking in the air. Air is good, we need air. We no longer need to suck anything else. Without fail, if you have a thought or idea of sucking, you will take in a deep breath, hold it for one, two, three, and let it out. Without fail, if the old thought of sucking your thumb would pop into your mind you know what to do.

So look into the future today, tomorrow, or perhaps a weekend. How will it be when you go to bed to sleep at night?" He reported everything looked great, he felt good about his brother and we ended the session.

Result: My last session with Tony was three weeks later and the sucking had stopped. He asked his mom to bring him for some hypnosis (he knew the name now!), because he wanted to be sure he never sucked again, especially as he was soon planning a sleepover with friends. We worked on having positive feelings for oral hygiene and dental visits also. His dentist reports Tony escaped the need for braces altogether and enjoys his dental visits.

CASE HISTORY 6: 44 year old Grinding Teeth – Regression to Cause

Mona's doctor referred her to the consulting hypnotist for headaches and jaw pain. She said she had been grinding her teeth "forever" and her right jaw was sore and giving her nerve pain which was worsened while opening and closing the jaw. She seemed to feel better in the warm Arabian Gulf climate, but the thoughts of returning to her native, colder country filled her with dread as "everything is worse there".

Regression to cause took us to age four, being touched in "uncomfortable places" by her father when he tucked her in at night. She would do all sorts of things to avoid him coming into her room but he continued and eventually sexually abused her. This continued for several years until there was another sibling who shared her room. Mona gnashed her teeth at the unfairness because her mother loved her father and could not see what he was doing. Mona felt angry because she felt she was protecting her mother and younger sister, who might be also be hurt by her father "if it weren't for me doing this". There was so much unsaid and that was the only way she could sleep or function because he said, "otherwise the words I need to say would drive me crazy." When I asked how she knew this, she whispered, "He told me he'd kill them if I didn't let him".

We had six sessions in all enabling her to forgive all the players in the drama using strategies such as Chair Therapy and Parts Therapy, while in hypnotic trance. Her symptoms were improving, she was no longer clenching during the day and grinding was reduced. Mona no longer wore her night guard. In the last two sessions, we worked from the discovery that the reason for her headaches recently, was the stress that her husband was possibly being transferred back to their home city. Her father was now elderly and sick, and in need of nursing care from Mona's mother. Mona feared she would be expected to help and she resented that her mother never realized Mona's sacrifice for her. Physical cold was not what made Mona's TMJ worse- it was the cold that she felt in her familial home. Continued grinding was because she wished to tell her husband, but she couldn't.

Result: Mona told her husband of 20 years about the sexual abuse and he was very supportive. He requested for any transfer that would not be to their home country and they went overseas again. Because of cultural considerations, Mona chose not to confide in her mother. When she spoke to her siblings they all said, "they kind of knew but didn't feel safe enough to say anything.' Her husband was very happy when they threw away the mouth guard. Mona is more secure in her marriage and no longer has facial pain or headaches. She wrote, "I feel like I have had a face lift. People say I look years younger. And, I am no longer an angry person inside so I don't grind my teeth. Thank you"

CASE HISTORY 7: 23 year old-Fear of Dentists – Fast Phobia Cure

John had graduated college and started a new job with a good insurance package and dental plan. He knew his teeth were in bad shape because he had not been to the dentist for ten years.

At age eight, the dentist had promised he would not hurt him and asked the "nurse" to hold him down because he was wriggling. He said there was pain but he could not remember it exactly and he had kicked the dentist in the stomach, although now as an adult he realized it may have been "lower down".

At age thirteen, John visited the dentist again. He had been terrified going to his last appointment, couldn't relax and wouldn't let the dentist use "gas" because of "I don't trust dentists, I want to know what they are doing". However, he wanted to take advantage of the dental plan and to look good as an executive and find a girlfriend who did not nag him about his teeth.

We discussed the previous events and he agreed he was much smaller, did not know what he knows now, and in retrospect nothing happened. As a rugby player, he was able to take some discomfort when he wanted an outcome- i.e. a goal.

He had seen many hypnosis stage shows and had asked a lot of questions about hypnosis, which I answered thoroughly. He agreed to go into hypnosis "because nothing else has worked for me". I told him he would be in control and we set up ideo-motor responses i.e. index finger for "yes", thumb for "no" and wiggling all fingers for "I don't know". He felt very relaxed about that!

I did a Dave Elman Induction (Elman Rapid Induction) as I felt this would give him more of a feeling of being in control. I deepened the trance by taking him on a journey inside his own brain, through all the layers of conscious and subconscious, wandering through all the parts and memories, tastes, smells and touches, thoughts and feelings etc. stored there in the organic computer. I asked him to be in wonderment and what a wonderful job the brain does protecting us, looking after us as the central processing unit. The brain will never knowingly destroy us, for in destroying us it destroys itself. Everything there is there to protect us (his ideo-motor responses all through were agreeing). I asked the subconscious mind if it would be willing to update the information stored there and then choose to use that information in any way it decides to protect John, response was "yes".

I used The Fast Phobia/Trauma Relief Technique described here. This technique neutralizes the powerful, negative feelings of phobias and traumatic events and can be a first level intervention with clients who "fear" regression. Most people learned to be phobic in a single situation that was actually dangerous, or seemed dangerous. The fact that individuals can do what psychologists call "one-trial learning" is proof that a person's brain can learn quite rapidly. That ability to learn rapidly makes it easy for you to learn a new way to respond to any phobia or trauma. The part of you that has been protecting you all these years by making you phobic is an important and valuable part. We want to preserve its ability to protect you in dangerous situations. The purpose of this technique is to refine and improve your brain's ability to protect you by updating its information.

"I want you to imagine walking into a movie theater, it is a new movie theater, and you can smell the new paint mixed with the smell of popcorn, you are alone and you feel very safe here. Find a seat in the middle of the movie theater, an ergonomically designed chair that molds to your body. Move around and feel very comfortable. As you take a warm, comfortable breath now, you are sitting in the middle of the theater and you look up and see a black and white snapshot of yourself on the screen. It has a big smile on your face.

Now, float out of your body and up into the projection booth. See yourself sitting in the movie theater seat and see the black and white photo on the screen so far away. You may even wish to imagine Plexiglas over the booth's opening, protecting you. There are many dials and switches here, they are all labeled and you know how to use them. The on and off switches: the pause and volume controls; the zoom in and zoom out.

Now, I will ask you to watch and listen, protected in the projection booth, as you see a black and white movie of a younger you going through that time you experienced that trauma. Watch the whole event - starting before the beginning when everything was okay. Observe until you are beyond the end of it, when everything was OKAY again. And let me know by raising your yes finger when it is all finished.

> *If you are not fully detached, make the theater screen smaller and farther away, make the picture grainier, stop and start the film so that when you're done viewing it, you're completely detached.*

> (When the yes finger rose) *I asked John to open his eyes and there on the screen right in front of him is the freeze frame picture of himself with a big grin on his face.*

Take a deep breath and SLEEP. (finger snap and catch head) *Now here you are in the projector room, leave the projection booth and slip back into the present- you in the theater seat feeling good. Now step into the freeze photo of the younger you, who is feeling OKAY again, at the movie's end.* (This is double dissociation.)

Now, run the entire movie of that experience backwards in color, taking two seconds or less to do so. Be sure to go all the way back to before the beginning. See, hear, and feel everything going backwards in those two seconds or less. Begin now.

To test the process, attempt to return to the fearful state in any way you can. Try to feel the way you used to and the more you try to feel the feelings you used to, the more you relax. What happened in the past has no effect on you. It is just historical events that have no effect on you, now.

What if you were in that situation now? When will you next encounter one of these situations? How is it going to be?

(Note to hypnotist: If you still get a phobic response, repeat the steps exactly, but faster each time, until none of the phobic (fearful) responses remains.)

*Since you were fearful (phobic), you have stayed far away from those particular situations in which you used to feel phobic, so you haven't had the opportunity to learn about them. Now you realize you are The Survivor, they probably named the TV program after you! As you begin to encounter and explore these situations in the future, you will choose well certified dentists to exercise a certain degree of caution until you learn to be more and more comfortable with them." (*Emerge*)

John felt great after hypnosis and was surprised how easy it had been although not quite sure what had happened. He said he felt good about making an appointment but still wanted another session because he couldn't believe he could get rid of this fear in one session (I have often experienced this with clients). When he returned for session two, he had already made a dental appointment. His only concern was that he wouldn't know what to do, and perhaps the dentist will tell him off for not looking after his teeth, when he had been very careful with oral hygiene to avoid dentists! We did a technique called The Grey Room (see script section) in which he took down his fears and excuses from his inner mind and other negative feelings and eliminated them.

Result: John is happily enjoying all the benefits of the dental plan and says going to the dentist is just a routine thing he does every six months.

CASE HISTORY 8: Surgery for Abscesses in the Mandible

A friend was going to have extensive work done on the lower right half of her mouth. In spite of pain, her schedule had caused her to put off seeing her dentist until there were abscesses in the mandible, extending from the midline and going all the way around the full right side. The procedure required was to make an incision from the front of the mandible all the way around the right side and then to scrape the bone clean. It was then to be stitched back together. It should be noted that this procedure was considered to most likely have a painful and swollen outcome.

I was unable to meet with her long enough to do pre-surgical conditioning, so I had to let some waking hypnosis suffice. I mentioned that she had chosen a good dentist, her surgery would go well and she would recuperate quickly. Following the surgery, after she filled her prescription for Percocet, she met me while her jaw was still numb from the surgery. I used a simple Elman induction and then had her work with me in visualizing the blood going into the area and bringing in all the healing elements needed and then washing away all unnecessary fluids and debris. I used several different imageries with her because I was new and unsure of how much to do. I figured I would rather do more than not enough.

There was a humorous side resulting from the guided imagery I used to reduce her inflammation. I did a series of imageries. The third one was about imagining clear, cool water just gently flushing the area clean, soothing and calming the area while washing away all debris and used fluids. She vaguely remembered the imagery during the night, when she awoke to a soaked pillowcase. Her body had been very busy washing the area clean. She had to get up and put a new dry pillowcase on her pillow as she chuckled to herself about the water she could faintly remember from the suggestions. Her thought was that it must be working, and she went back to sleep.

Result: There never was any swelling and not only was the Percocet unnecessary, she did not require anything at all for pain. She healed so rapidly that the oral surgeon opted not to pull the stitches out on her one-week check-up. He had used dissolving stitches and felt it best not to disturb the healing of the gums.

Although I would have preferred to pre-condition her for the surgery as well, I was able to get right back to her afterwards and the result was amazing to her and her oral surgeon.

CASE HISTORY 9: Anxiety & Grinding Teeth

Simone age 13

Jaw clenching or teeth grinding can make a disorder of the TMJ joint more likely. When the joint is overworked, a disc in the joint can wear down or move out of place. Grinding and clenching also can change the alignment of the bite (the way that top and bottom teeth line up) and can affect muscles used for chewing. Simone did not even realize that she was clenching or grinding and even doing it during her sleep.

Stress can make kids more likely to grind their teeth, clench their jaw, or tighten their jaw muscles, and this was the case for Simone who had symptoms of clenching since moving to a new city and new school. Her parents now lived in two different countries with her father travelling from their troubled country to visit once per month, her elder brother at boarding school in another country for intense language skills pre-university. Simone had lost everything and everyone she loved except her mother who now felt much like a stranger in their new land as she now worked away from home (a new concept for Simone).

According to teachers, Simone was clenching during the day and upon observing more her mother saw she was doing so at night also. Normally a quiet, sensitive and intelligent child who never complained she had pain in her right facial muscles, jaw joints, as well as around the right ear, neck and shoulders. She had pain when talking and chewing and had begun yawning to avoid muscle spasms and the popping, clicking, grating sounds she said she heard when opening or closing her mouth. Recently she had been taken to the doctor for headaches, dizziness and ear pain. She had been checked for migraines and hearing loss and diagnosed with anxiety and grinding of teeth resulting in some misalignment of her jaws. Consequently, she had been on a soft foods diet, avoiding chewing gum and other foods which further isolated her at school as a teen. Mother said it was hard to stop nagging Simone about clenching her jaw or grinding which made their relationship tense. Simone spent evenings with ice packs or heat to the side of her face to feel more comfortable and often took medication to help relieve the pain and relax the muscles.

The dentist had talked to Simone about fitting a splint or biteplate to wear at night to help reduce clenching and grinding. He said he wanted to avoid surgery to repair damaged tissue in the joint and referred her for hypnotherapy.

PreTalk: We talked about the different levels of brain reviewing the mind model in Beryl's YouTube clip which client viewed before coming. Simone preferred to use the term "magic mind" instead of "unconscious" as she wanted the magic to "make me better so I don't have to wear a splint or braces". We talked about all the stresses in her life (as above) and whether the teeth thing made it better or worse. She knew Mum was under a lot of pressure and didn't know how to talk to her daughter, and felt guilty about being a problem for her. We looked at some ways she could communicate better and what activities would be better to do than getting anxious.

Induction: I used an Elman Induction and Simone lost numbers quickly. I used a gentle form of parts therapy for the first session with ideo-motor responses. As follows:

Lots of kids develop pain in their jaw as a result of unconsciously grinding their teeth or clenching the jaw over and over again. Some kids then have to wear braces which they hate, or only eat soft food (no burgers, imagine that!). How sad. Maybe you know that you've been clenching and grinding, maybe you don't know. But your magic mind (your unconscious) knows everything about you and what you do. Even when you're asleep! As a very famous man once said, "when you know better, you do better".

Today we are talking to your magic mind. When you're breathing even deeper and feeling relaxed and ready to talk to your magic mind, please let one of your fingers, your "yes" finger come up, all by itself. (Wait for response)

Thank you magic mind. And which finger would be a "no" finger? (Wait for response)

Magic mind, I want you to scan through Simone's days (like scanning through a movie from beginning to end on rewind) - for example, during a test at school, when angry, worried or upset, asleep or awake, alone or with others - and notice when she chews or grinds her teeth, look for all the times. When you know them all please raise the "yes" finger.

Thank you. Now please let Simone know when these times are. So she knows. And when she knows them all, please raise the "yes" finger.

Thank you. Magic mind would you be willing to help Simone to control these habits by making her instantly notice these behaviors when they happen so you can consciously stop them? Yes or no?

Thank you magic mind. Now, there's always something better to do than grind teeth and then have to spend lots of time putting that right. So I want you to find five things Simone can do instead of that old grinding behavior. And give me a yes signal for every one you find. I'll count. (Pause while this happens and count as the finger is raised)

Thank you magic mind. If the behavior is a result of stress, can you help Simone get plenty of exercise to release all that nervous energy?

Can you help Simone to breathe nice and deep – and let that breath out nice and slow - when she is nervous and needs to relax.

Magic mind will all these changes work for Simone? Will you help? Thank you.

Anything else that needs to be done today? (If so I would deal with it, and emerge)

There were no issues so I emerged her. Afterwards Simone asked if she could see me again to work on her some other feelings her magic mind asked her to trust me with. The underlying feelings were guilt at being the reason mum had to leave dad alone in a tense situation. We did some chair therapy in hypnosis in a second session, as well as further sessions on anger at the people who did bad things in her country. Then a session on becoming one of the girls and allowing herself to have fun without guilt nor fear of others' judgement.

Simone says she has reduced her grinding by 80% within two weeks. She now knows when it is happening and is able to stop it. She went to the cinema with girlfriends and is looking forward to a sleepover after exams. She Skypes her brother each week and both enjoy speaking their native language together. We agreed to meet again in six months and review her situation and she has my CD to listen to whenever she wants extra relaxation and assurance.

CASE HISTORY 10: Lucy Grinding her Teeth

Lucy, 33 from Eastern Europe was overcome with anxiety and grinding her teeth while she slept. Although a highly qualified engineer, she now lived outside of her native country with her husband and child as a non-working wife. She felt lonely and isolated as her English language skills were not good enough for employment and her social skills with other housewives were minimal. Despite what she said, I found her language skills very good and easy to conduct a pre-talk and for her to follow a modified Elman Induction.

I decided to use parts therapy. I was able to talk to the part of her subconscious that was generating the anxiety. I asked the part for "its name, and what its job is. She replied, that it was the part that warns of danger. When I asked why it was making her so anxious, I was told that it was her fear of being alone and of the unknown. I asked if there was something happening that contributed to that fear and the part answered, "my husband". Further examination of the part found that her husband was always putting her down, expecting her to spend time with her community yet not talking English with her. She felt frustrated because she wanted to learn and go to classes where she would meet other interesting people, but her husband was jealous and said she must not leave the child alone so she can go to school.

I knew I could not change her husband, but I explained that I could help her control her reaction to him - would that be OK with the part? So, I deepened the hypnosis then to **ultra-height**. (A level and strategy designed by Gerald Kein) and asked the part to listen in while I spoke to another part. I touched her on the forehead and asked to speak to the creative part - the smart solutions part. I asked that part to analyze the situation and all her life and come up with one to three solutions that would work for her so she could take control of her reactions to this situation now.

The part said it had two new ways of reacting. I asked if these were good for Lucy and the environment she lived in, and it replied yes. I took her further into ultra-height and asked if there were any "energies" around to help her, she found her deceased aunt there who said she would always be there for her and give her patience and focus to learn English. I asked her to look into the future and asked if there was anything stopping her. She answered "nothing." I asked her to scan her body and ask if all parts of mind, body and spirit agreed with the negotiations and changes. They did. I asked would she ever need to grind her teeth again and the answer was "no".

I brought her back to somnambulism and did some direct suggestion as learned from Don Mottin. *You are going to be very pleased to discover that letting go of the habit of grinding your teeth is very simple for you now. Teeth grinding has been a behavior, a habit that you've been doing subconsciously. Through the use of this hypnosis session today, the habit has gone.*

You have control over your mind and body. At this very moment, if I asked you to, you could move your hands and place them on your legs, simply by deciding to do so. If I asked you to, you could move your hands and you could place them on your stomach, simply by deciding to do so. In fact, if I asked you to, you could move your hands and place them on top of your head, simply by deciding to do so. Of course, if I asked you to, you could relax your jaw muscles and, if your teeth are clenched together, unclench them. Do that now - so, you have control over the movements of your body.

From this moment on, if you begin the habit or cycle of grinding your teeth, you will become aware of it instantly and you will stop the behavior. If you ever begin grinding your teeth again, you will notice it immediately, and you will stop the behavior. You will stop grinding your teeth.

You have control over the movements of your jaw. You have control over the movements of your entire body. It is now becoming impossible for you to begin to grind your teeth without being consciously aware of the behavior. Allow your teeth to begin to touch now as if they were starting to grind, and notice that feeling. You will become aware of that feeling if it ever occurs again. So, without fail, without exception, without excuse, if you begin to grind your teeth, you will become aware of it instantly, your jaw muscles will relax, and the behavior will stop instantly.

It is now totally and completely an impossibility for you to grind your teeth without being consciously aware. And, since you have made a conscious and unconscious decision to stop this behavior, and all parts agree, you will never, ever grind your teeth again"

Result: She has been free of the grinding problem ever since. We had another session, not so long afterwards, and did the grey room technique and focused her confidence in meeting people and talking English and she began looking for a job. At a language group, she met a British engineer who wanted to learn her language for an assignment in her country, and they were helping each other.

CASE 11: General Anxiety and Fear of Needles

James, 39 was a successful expat living and working overseas. He stated that he has had general anxiety and fear of needles all his life,. He had avoided doctors and dentists and now his teeth were in such a state that a lot of major work was required. And, he was terrified.

The first session he was even anxious about hypnosis although I had sent him information beforehand. I explained how hypnosis works after going through the intake form with him. We worked out a plan together which made him feel as though he had some control. First session would be to see how "good" he could be at hypnosis as he was wary about whether he could relax (although I explain to people that is my job to help them, they still want to help"). I demonstrated with the "stiff arm test" that trying is not doing, and asked him to promise **not to try** to relax ... he laughed! We did hypnosis using a Rapid Dave Elman Induction and he was soon in trance. I brought him out, put him in again three times – each time deeper. (Fractionation) He was loving it! I quickly taught him how to "turn off" sensations and create numbness (analgesia) when he wanted to, for any area he chose.

Second session, calling it "Time Line Work" we did regression to cause of the anxiety and fear. Seven months in fetus (i.e. in the womb), he felt the same fear. I asked, "If you knew where that was coming from where would that be?" It was his mother worrying because she was taking drugs through needle injection; she was in a hospital bed and worrying about losing her baby, feeling guilty. James almost died and although a fetus understood that, the needles had caused him to be so sick. It was easy for him to resolve the problem for he now knew that the anxiety was from his mother, about her life. And the fear was because he almost died in the womb.

I asked him to give the infant the knowledge that he would survive and be okay. Then I asked him to give his mother the knowledge that this information would enable her to take better care of her child. I then asked him to review his life's timeline from that point on and use that new knowledge, in whatever way was appropriate, to heal what he had come in to see me for. He forgave his mother as she had been a good mother and had quit taking drugs for his sake.

At the end of this second session, I had him scan his body for any fear and used a pre-surgery script to give him confidence. When emerged he said he felt "terrific", even though this was the first time as an adult he had spoken about his mother's previous addiction. He felt as though "a weight has been removed' for all the mixture of guilt and fear he had felt if the "truth" ever came out.

Result: Third session, James had been to the dentist and had a shot. There was some general anxiety but he felt great and empowered. We strengthened the anchor for his numbness feelings by talking directly to the anxious part (Parts Therapy) and it searched for five new behaviors or beliefs to satisfy its good intention then threw away the old behavior. Lastly, I used a short ego-strengthening script and future pacing so he could see himself going through all the subsequent surgeries. He felt a lot better and when I asked him to "try and feel the feeling you used to get about needles," he could not. When I asked him to "really try, like he used to", he laughed and we both knew he would be in control of his reactions from this point onwards whenever at the dentist.

CASE 12: Gagging over Dentures

Ibtisam was referred by her dentist because she was not accepting her new top row dentures, unable to keep them in place because wanted to vomit. In addition, the dentist was unable to take an impression for the bottom row dentures due to gagging. As a confident school administrator who had brought up her daughter alone following a bad marriage and divorce, Ibtisam was very embarrassed about this problem, as well as a bit skeptical how hypnosis would help. She admitted to feeling a bit frightened of failure that she "might not be able to do it (i.e. hypnosis)" and brought her daughter with her for support.

Following a thorough pre-talk, we established the goal for session one to be: a) able to relax putting in the dentures which she already had without gagging and b) keep them in for a minimum of four hours and maybe longer each day for the next four days. I used a gentle version of the Elman induction and I was not convinced that she had lost the numbers, so I deepened her using a wandering along the beach while further losing numbers drawn in the sand. Following direct suggestions for relaxation and asking her subconscious mind if was willing to update information today and then decide what to do with it, I had her view all excuses for fear of failure and consider whether she wanted to continue thinking in a way that she wasn't born to feel. We ended with a post hypnotic suggestion to go instantly into hypnosis on her next visit and even deeper. Her daughter said she also "fell asleep while watching her mother doing hypnosis and felt good".

For our second meeting, Ibtisam came alone. She reported feeling much more relaxed and wearing her dentures most of the day. She removed the dentures in the evenings, but was confident that in the following days she would be wearing them all day. We set that as a goal for this session adding that she would make an appointment for having the lower jaw impressions made. When I asked how she felt about that, she said she felt "sick to her stomach".

Following an instant induction, I brought up the feeling she had when she was at the dentist and the dentist was touching her bottom jaw. I had her intensify the feeling when he was taking an impression to the point just before she vomited. When I asked her mind to go back to the first time she had that feeling, she regressed to a childhood sexual abuse issue she had never told to anyone. Her distress was evident so I took her through that quickly, knowing she would survive. We brought in older Ibtisam to tell her child self that all was ok, and that she was safe and secure. We went before the incident so she could go through again knowing she would survive and that the items in her mouth could not hurt her and she could breathe. This was done a few times with Ibtisam yelling out her truth until she had no emotion going through the event. We then did forgiveness of the perpetrator, and forgave others for being unapproachable to listen. Then we worked on forgiveness of self for feeling the way she had, for the guilt and shame and not telling...reinforcing the fact that she was not at fault.

When she arrived for her third session, I hardly recognized Ibtisam because she looked so relaxed. She had been for a massage and facial, things she had never done before, as she hated people touching her. She had booked her appointment with her dentist for taking an impression for her bottom jaw dentures. I did a body scan and was given permission to send energy wherever it was required and then the grey room script (see script section).

Result: Ibtisam has had a wonderful complete set of dentures for several years now, and loves them.

CASE 13: Older Gentleman with Fear of a Medical Procedure.

This widowed gentleman in his late 70's with children, lived alone and his general health was good. He was phobic of dentists and injections and was due to undergo a procedure involving taking biopsies from growths on the tongue and jaw, and he was scared.

Referred to me by another client, he phoned to make an appointment explaining that he did not really believe in hypnotherapy but was willing to try anything. He was also extremely well-mannered, courteous, articulate, and educated being a retired scientist with a very analytical mind.

His purpose in seeking help was to assist him to attend the hospital for a day surgery procedure where biopsies were to be taken from his tongue and jaw area. The procedure was to be done under local anesthetic and scheduled in a couple of weeks. When he had gone to the initial appointment, he had suffered massive anxiety attacks requiring several staff to hold him down in order for the preliminary examination to take place. Even the thought of going near the hospital was causing severe anxiety and the thought of the procedure was causing visible excessive perspiration.

In the first session, a full history of the client was conducted to ensure that the client details were accurate and that there were no serious medical issues that could contra-indicate the use of hypnosis for the client; hypnosis and states of mind were explained in detail. Due to the age of the client and the short time scale in which to work, I decided to use metaphors and suggestion therapy to deal with the presenting problem.

The session was conducted consisting of general relaxation and healing intervention which included teaching the client self-hypnosis via a physical anchor- finger and thumb rub. After this, the client commented that he did not feel hypnotized but did feel relaxed. A further appointment was arranged.

In the second session, a confusion induction was used to bypass the conscious critical faculty, followed by suggestions for physical relaxation. The session concentrated mainly on visualizations of the hospital visit, the procedure, giving positive suggestions that the whole episode would pass quickly, and that he was able to work with the hospital staff and be acquiescent to the instructions and requirements of the staff. Further, that he would remain calm and relaxed before and during the visit and, subsequently, would heal very quickly with minimum discomfort. The "Glove Technique" was taught to the client for pain management, so that he could imagine the whole area was numb even before being given any local anesthetic. Suggestions were given for him to be almost oblivious of what was happening and he would barely even notice what the doctors were doing unless his attention was required.

In the third session, a long physical relaxation was repeated, allied to the finger-thumb anchor to relax the client and teach him to use the anchor and be able to relax the various parts of the body. A metaphor was introduced that involved a story of an animal that was afraid of sharp branches in the forest. The animal was gradually introduced to various types of branches and trees, some were sharp, some were blunt, and the animal learned how to manage the different types of pressure and touch and that some were even quite pleasant to experience. The animal met an owl, and the owl taught him to fly and as part of this, the animal could fly far up away from all the things that could upset him. While doing this, it was almost as if he were looking at himself feeling relaxed and comfortable and undergoing experiences that would make his life better. It was a very esoteric metaphor with lots of minor stories within it all around the animal being worried and concerned and when he actually did what was needed, the experience was much easier than he ever imagined it could be. In addition, when he was injured, he found that he recovered very quickly and easily.

In the fourth and final session, a garden visualization was used as an induction (it was suggested that the client could imagine this garden when he wanted to relax or disassociate from any situation). The finger to thumb anchor was again reinforced to gain instant relaxation and calmness. Another "walk through" of the planned event was done in hypnotic trance. Some more little metaphors were introduced, this time about a fish, who had damaged its mouth and was then caught on a hook. The fish was terrified, but when the angler lifted him out of the water and took the hook out, somehow the angler removed the damaged part of the mouth and put the fish back in the water. To his amazement, after a short time, the fish's mouth felt so much better, and he was grateful to the angler who had frightened him at first but then cured him etc. Again fast healing suggestions were given along with confidence and self-esteem boosters.

As my client left for the final time, he said, "Thank you so much. It has been very nice, not sure that I have actually been hypnotized but I do feel relaxed. I'll let you know how I get on."

Result: A few weeks later, I had a phone call from the client. "Thought I'd let you know, it all went well, I was not at all bothered, can't understand why I was worried. It was a shame that I was not able to be hypnotized, but I did enjoy the sessions." This was from the man who had freaked out even at the thought of going to the hospital, and was phobic about anything being put in his mouth!

It is amazing how so common this response can be. Even though hypnosis has been explained fully, with the effects (or not), the perception can still be there that they were not hypnotized. The positive outcome is obviously "just a coincidence".

Section 6:

SAMPLE OF SCRIPTS

FOR CONSULTING HYPNOTISTS & DENTISTS

A WORD ON SCRIPTS

Scripts are a guide, not the last word. We recommend you realize that "the client is the script". S/he (and the dental practitioner) tells you, the consulting hypnotist, everything you need to know when you listen carefully: ie. Their motivation, goal, problem and expected outcome. It is our job to listen, educate, reassure and make change consistent with their outcome using the most effective tools available to us: regression to cause, parts therapy, inner child work, hypnotic anesthesia, self-hypnosis, positive suggestion etc.

The Hypnotist is advised to practice a script and become familiar with its components before using it with a client. Scripts will need change depending on the client's issues and their changes occurring since the last appointment, time of day etc. The script may not be appropriate in its entirety during a session, however sections may be very empowering when integrated with other associated suggestions. In other words, a script provides an excellent launch into responses that are more intuitive. Our day by day intuitional level is not always as sharp as we might like it to be. When faced with special challenges, scripts help us in those situations when we seem to "draw a blank."

No one can memorize all the scripts, nor is there enough time in a day to construct one script for each individual client on a busy daily basis. Nor, conversely, is it wise to restrict yourself to only one, two, or three scripts memorized comfortably. We are working with our clients' map of their world, not our own (with which we are comfortable). Keeping this in mind, become conversant with a wide variety of suggestions and imagery that you can draw on depending on the areas of concern your client has identified. For example if a pain is hot, change it to cool, throbbing to soothing – ask them, they will tell you what they want!

An experienced Consulting Hypnotist may have three to five references open before them during the active part of a session. When regressing, even though you are very familiar with the technique, you might want to use specific vs. general wording. During the same hypnosis session, you may conclude that switching to some Parts Therapy work becomes more applicable, or determine that a particular turn of phrase fits with the client's own wording or stated philosophy, and then your resources are readily available.

The alternative is relying on memory, and then perhaps misstating embedded objectives. In other words; flying by the seat of your pants is ineffective, and inefficient guidance.

Having said that, if you are employing parts, regression, or affect bridge, etc., you, as the consulting hypnotist, must be familiar with not only the techniques, but their accompanying phraseology and intended applicability too. Others, who have gone before us, have provided a solid groundwork of understanding of hypnotherapeutic techniques, which are largely based on common sense. The most useful source of information here is Dave Elman: "Hypnotherapy" and Banyan & Kein: "Hypnosis and Hypnotherapy" and practical DVDs on regression work available from www.omnihypnosis.com

That still means though that you must read, read, and read more scripts along with the underlying script reasoning and philosophy so you can serve your client's best interests. Carefully worded suggestions, in script form, help avoid the trap of unintentionally using language that may be less than helpful.

However, we believe without question that your inductions should be memorized. Whether using Elman Inductions, Chalkboard Technique for analytical resistors or Dr. Flowers for the kinesthetic, the idea is to bypass the critical factor. If the conscious mind is reflecting, *"Wow, that voice is really soothing, and it really seems to know what it's talking about,"* then you can guide your client into somnambulism quicker and more easily.

However, if the practitioner is rustling paper, hesitating, stuttering and delivering an uneasy indu

ction, the conscious mind notices and distrust holds back cooperation. Then the client may have to be shocked or confused, or the session terminated.

Once past the critical factor, although the subconscious will pick up your voice whether you speak quickly, slowly, in a quiet, high or in an excited voice, you can maximize subconscious absorption, whether direct suggestions or Ericksonian, by "living" the script.

In other words, believe in the script. Say the words with meaning, with expression and with a wholehearted confidence, rather than by bored rote. Although you do not have to convince the subconscious to listen to you (it is always listening anyway), it will accept your suggestions even more readily if you yourself believe what you're saying, and the preference is to deliver while your client is in the somnambulistic state.

Also, remember that the conscious is always present to some extent. Although minimized and off to the side to some extent, it can still judge your "performance" when returned to normal consciousness (beta). This could affect the rate and degree of absorption depending on judged credibility.

Scripts are found under heading indicators:

    Inductions (A)

    Deepeners (B)

    Suggestions and Reinforcers (C)

    Emerging (D)

ELMAN / KEIN HAND DROP INSTANT INDUCTION (A)

NOTE: This induction is best seen in Gerald Kein's DVD "Instant and Rapid Inductions"

"Place your hand in mine…. Like that – got it? (their hand is placed on hypnotist's upturned palm)

Now, look at me – right here (point to your forehead).

At the count of three, press down continuously against my hand.

I'll be pressing up against your power …… got it?

Now, follow my instructions completely…. OK?

One   (wagging your finger at the subject with each count)

Two, three….. PUSH, PUSH, PUSH. That's right ….. push hard, that's good.

Now, let your eyes become heavy, droopy,,, drowsy and sleepy …. Closing ... closing ...

(If you have to, pull the subject's eyelids shut with your thumb and index finger.)

(Now, instantly pull your hand out from under the subject's and say "SLEEP" and tap the subject on the forehead with the palm of your hand.)

As I rock your head gently, allow your body to go loose and limp and deeply relaxed. Every breath guiding you deeper relaxed.

As I lift your head allow the movement to guide you deeper relaxed and allow your neck to hold your head quite comfortably.

(Do a five to one count down for eye catalepsy, deepen and test for depth)

CONFUSION INDUCTION METHOD (A)

The basic message to this induction is the conscious forgetting, and the subconscious knowing. Separate directions for the conscious mind, and separate directions for the subconscious mind maintain the subconscious attention, while dismissing the conscious attention both by the suggestions and the pauses and mental fatigue. Read the text slowly and rhythmically.

(Read once, don't repeat) Just close your eyelids and let your mind drift where it will.

You are aware of everything, and yet you are not aware. You are listening with your subconscious mind, while your conscious mind is far away, and not listening. Your conscious mind is far away, and not listening. Your subconscious mind is awake, and listening, and hearing everything while your conscious mind remains very relaxed and peaceful. You can relax peacefully because your subconscious mind is taking charge, and when this happens, you close your eyes and let your subconscious do all the listening. Your subconscious mind knows, and because your subconscious mind knows, your conscious mind does not need to know and can stay asleep, and not mind while your subconscious mind stays wide awake.

You have much potential in your subconscious mind which you don't have in your conscious mind. You can remember everything that has happened with your subconscious mind, but you cannot remember everything with your conscious mind. You can forget so easily, and with forgetting certain things, you can remember other things. Remembering what you need to remember, and forgetting what you can forget. It does not matter if you forget, you need not remember.

Your subconscious mind remembers everything that you need to know and you can let your subconscious mind listen and remember while your conscious mind sleeps and forgets. Keep your eyes closed, and listen with your subconscious mind, and when you are listening very, very carefully, your head can nod "yes".

As you continue to listen to me, with your subconscious mind, your conscious mind sleeps deeper and deeper, and deeper, and deeper. Let your conscious mind stay deeply asleep, and let your subconscious mind listen to me. *(Repeat paragraph two, deepen and test)*

DEEPENING: Wave (B)

Your arms are loose and limp, just like a rag doll. As I raise your hand, just let the entire weight hang limply in my fingers. And, when I drop it, send a wave of relaxation all across your body. As you feel your hand touch your body, send that wave of relaxation from the top of your head all the way down to the very tips of your toes.

And, as you do, you find that you double your previous level of relaxation.

Now, once again, with the other hand. (Repeat with other hand)

DEEPENING: Staircase Method (B)

Note: check for allergies to feathers before using this!

In a moment, I'm going to relax you more completely. In a moment, I'm going to begin counting backwards from 10 to 1.... As I say the number 10 you will allow your eyelids to become heavier and heavier. And as I say the number 10, I want you, in your mind's eye, to imagine as if you are at the top of a small set of stairs, safe and secure.

The moment I say the number 9, and each additional number, you will simply allow yourself to move down those stairs easily and effortlessly, relaxing more completely. At the base of the stairs is a large feather bed, with a comfortable feather pillow. You are really looking forward to being there, curled up and cozy, safe and secure. The moment I say the number one, you will simply sink into that bed, resting your head on that feather pillow.

Number 10, eyes closed at the top of those stairs. Ten ...
9... relaxing and letting go. Nine ...
8... sinking softly into a more comfortable, calm, peaceful position ...
7 ... very safe ... safe and secure
6 ... going way down ... deeper
5 ... moving down those stairs ... relaxing more completely.
4 ... and 3 ... breathe in deeply...
2 ... on the next number, number one, simply sinking into that bed, becoming more calm, more peaceful, more relaxed ...
1 ... sinking into that feather bed, let every muscle go limp and loose as you sink into a more calm, peaceful state of relaxation.

DEEPENING 2: (B) Sleep Now Fractionation

I am going to give you a signal so you can enter into hypnosis more easily.

I am going to count from one to three. At the count of three, you will open your eyes, remaining deeply relaxed. When I say "Sleep now" and snap my fingers, that will be the signal for your eyelids to close down and you will go deeper into hypnosis.

All right. One. Two. Three. Open your eyes. (*Snap finger*)   Sleep Now!
Close them down and go deeper asleep. (Repeat both several times)

DEEPENER AND TREATMENT FOR ANXIETY (B) & (C)

Induction of choice followed by.....

"Imagine as if, now, you're standing outside - in the moonlight at the top of a lovely stairway, and it's a lovely warm summer's night. The stairway is made of white marble and is lit all the way down with lamp lights. You can see the stairs are wide and they wind gently down, and at the bottom of the stairs is a lovely pool.

As you look down the stairs, you notice there are twenty steps leading gently down. These are the stairs which will take you deep into relaxation. Deep into hypnosis. You begin to walk down the stairs, counting with me...... 20 ... (*Count down to zero in time with client's exhale*).

And now, you're standing at the bottom of the stairs and you notice a beautiful pool. Floating on top of the water are thousands of rose petals. The fragrance from the roses is very heady and you bend down to lift a petal, noticing the velvety softness on your fingertips.

The water is very warm and inviting and so you lower yourself into the water and float along on a bed of rose petals. Just imagine your body floating on a bed of rose petals, across this beautiful pool.

The water supports your body. Feel your body, bobbing gently up and down, up and down - imagine it - experience it now. Continue floating along, really enjoying this wonderful feeling. (Pause).

Let yourself drift and float, drift and float, relaxing more and more with each breath that you take - for with each breath that you take and with each word that is uttered - this wonderful floating feeling fills you with a mixture of calm and tranquility - and you find yourself drifting - floating - to a wonderful, safe, relaxing place.

And as you are floating here, safe and relaxed - it doesn't matter if, from time to time, you find your mind beginning to wander to other thoughts and feelings, because nobody wants anything, nobody needs anything - there is absolutely nothing of any importance for you to do, but relax, and let go.

Feel the warmth of the air on your body, calming your body, relaxing your body, making it feel even more tranquil, even more peaceful, and even more comfortable than you can ever remember feeling. .... This wonderfully calm, relaxing feeling - as you float along - on this wonderful pool of peace.

Imagine the sky is becoming even darker now, remember, or allow yourself to think of, a warm, sultry, summer night. The air is filled with the delicate perfume of the rose petals - perhaps other flowers too -

night scented stock, geraniums – and the perfume reaches your nostrils, making you feel even more comfortable, even more calm, even more relaxed.

In the dark, velvety sky is a full, round moon, surrounded by twinkling, silvery stars. Everything here is so peaceful, everything here is so relaxing, everything here is so calming - and you take into yourself this calm - this relaxing - this peaceful feeling - experience it now - this calm, and peaceful, relaxing feeling. See how good it makes you feel.

As you gaze up into the velvet sky, on this calm and peaceful night, I want you to think of the word - peace - just allow yourself to think and feel the meaning of the word peace. The word peace. Because from now on, whenever you want to feel free from anxiety… whenever you want to feel as calm and relaxed and as peaceful as you feel right no… all you need to do is to close your eyes for one moment and think of your peaceful star, up there in the beautiful night sky, looking down on your floating body in your pool of peace.

And all those worries and anxieties that have been spoiling your life, will seem so insignificant, will just fade away, as once again you fill your entire body with peaceful feelings.

So listen carefully to me, very carefully, and remember - whenever you want to feel as calm as this again, all you need to do is close your eyes for a moment and think and feel the word peace. Peace. It's only a little word, but it has such beneficial effects. Peace. And you will find, that you will immediately feel, so much calmer, so much more tranquil, and so much more peaceful - just like you do at this moment in time. ….. Peaceful. ….

Okay now I want you to count up to five in your mind, and when you reach the number five, just open your eyes and feel refreshed and relaxed, and remember this wonderful peaceful feeling".

GENERAL PAIN MANAGEMENT SCRIPT 1 (C)

Induction of choice …. Check for somnambulism … followed by…..

"You know and I know and the doctors you know that there is one answer that you know that you don't want to know and that I know but don't want to know, that

Your family knows but doesn't want to know,   no matter how much you want to say no, you know that the no is really a yes, and you wish it could be a good yes and so do you know that what you and your family know is yes, yet they still wish it were no.

And just as you wish there were no pain, you know that there is but what you don't know is no pain is something you can know. And no matter what you knew, no pain would be better than what you know and of course what you want to know is no pain and that is what you are ...

Going to know, no pain... *(all of this is said slowly but with utter intensity and with seemingly total disregard of any interruption of cries of pain or admonitions of "shut up")*. You used to know pain and know no pain and so do you wish to know

No pain but comfort and you do know comfort and no pain and as comfort increases you know that   you cannot say no to ease and comfort but you can say no pain and

know no pain but you can say no pain and know no pain but know comfort and ease and it is so good to know comfort and ease and relaxation and to know it now and later and still longer and longer   as more and more relaxation occurs and to know it now and later and

Still longer and longer as more and more and more relaxation and wonderment and surprise come to your mind as you begin to know a freedom and a comfort you have so greatly desired and as you feel it

Grow and grow you know, really know, that today, to-night, tomorrow, all next week and all next month, and at your 13th birthday, and what a time that was, and those wonderful feelings that   you had then seem almost as clear as if they were today and the memory of every good thing is a glorious thing ".

As you begin to know a   freedom and a comfort you have so greatly desired and as you feel it grow and grow you know, really know, that today, to-night, tomorrow, all next week and all next month, and at the doctors and dentists and what a time that was,

And those wonderful feelings that you had then seem almost as clear as if they were today and the   memory of every good thing is a glorious thing ".

As you begin to know a freedom and a comfort you have so greatly desired and as you feel it

GENERAL DENTAL SCRIPT 2 (C)

Induction of choice .... Check for somnambulism ... followed by.....

We're going to start the work so you can remain calm, confident and in control in the dentist's chair. You have chosen to be in control, in control of your reaction to those things going on around you in the dental chair, Is that right? You are taking control of a situation that has been controlling you – true or false? (*Wait for response*) Wonderful, so it is.

When you are in the dentist's office, calling the dentist office, thinking of his/her office, procedures or anything connected with the dentist you experience total physical detachment from all physical feeling. You choose to be free, they are no concern of yours, and as your dentist works on you, you find you become calmer, relaxed, serene and from now on you are going to realize your mind creates your own reality.

In the past, you thought your dentist appointment had to be one of discomfort, which is therefore what you expected. Now you know many times in your life when you expect to do something and that's the way it was. When you expect to feel something, that's what you felt. From now on your expectation of your visit to the dentist office is going to be one of calm confidence. You know there is no reason to feel any discomfort with a well-trained dentist with all the technology and techniques available to them now.

So you notice the oddest thing happens. When you drive or are taken to your dental appointment with each mile you get closer. The closer you get to your dentist office the calmer and calmer and more and more confident you become, knowing that your visit heals you, and makes you feel better, tension-free and comfortable. Because you are in charge, in control of your feelings, in control of your reactions to those things, situations, people around you no longer control you, as you are in control of your reactions each and every day, relaxed in your knowledge you tell your feelings what they will feel and you are taking control NOW..

When you go into the dentist office and when you sit in the dentist chair instantly, as you lean back in that chair and your head hits that headrest, a wonderful feeling of calm and confidence flows from your head to your toes. Every muscle of your body relaxes in a wonderful anticipation of a positive, good experience. You are going to find that when the dentist comes in and you see the dentist you feel confident with him or her and your muscles stay calm and relaxed.

If that was all you were going to do, your dentist would be well pleased. You no longer feel any discomfort. Discomfort is eliminated. And you feel calm, confident and in control.

"You are with a professional and listen, sometimes you want to ask some questions and that's OK. You ask how long the procedure is, and if there may be some bleeding involved. You give yourself that time and that is the time you tell your body, the bleeding stops, and it stops. Instantly. It will stop and when I say instantly that means with 15 seconds. If s/he doesn't give instructions, you will set that anesthesia free and no bleeding, no discomfort of any kind. You go through your day naturally without any chemicals at all."

If sometimes the dentist wants to work on your mouth, and uses Novocain or something similar, s/he's going to give you little of a chemical to cause that part of your mouth to feel wonderful. And, you are going to find that as the dentist gives you that chemical you're so relaxed and confident you don't even notice what s/he's doing and how s/he is doing it... Because you are so relaxed and comfortable.

So ..."X"... when you go to the dentist, you're finding that you're going to feeling more and more confident, relaxed each and every day ... so great and proud.... that you are calm and confident and in control throughout the whole appointment and you feel wonderful. ....*EMERGE*

GLOVE ANESTHESIA - PAIN CONTROL SCRIPT (C)

Induction of choice .... Check for somnambulism ... followed by.....

The first thing that I would like you to do is to raise one of your hands up to about your chin height. Focus your attention on the hand that you raised. Feel the sensations in that hand. Imagine a tingling sensation beginning with the little finger on that hand. You can even separate the fingers slightly and raise the little finger up above the others, as if you were in the old English times and holding a cup of tea. Imagine a tingling sensation beginning in that finger. As if it was electrically charged or about to go to sleep. We all know how that feels, when we have slept on top of a hand and it feels numb the next morning. This is the same sensation.

There is a pulsing, tingling sensation in that finger. Your little finger is becoming quite numb and the numb feeling spreads to the ring finger... raise the ring finger up too. It tingles, feeling funny. Again the numbness spreads and the third finger feels numb, too. Tingling or feeling a course of electricity through it. Nod your head if you know what I mean . . . Good. Now the next finger, in fact all the fingers on that hand feel tingly. The tingle spreads to the palm and back of the hand. Take a moment, breathe, and as you exhale, notice the feelings as the hand is beginning to feel numb. You can even take your other hand and tap gently on the back of this one.

You are feeling for numb spots as you gently drum your fingers on the back of the hand that we have been focusing on. When you can numb your hand, you can transfer this numbness to any other part of your body. Do that now, for example, on your thigh, your leg. Place the numb hand on your leg and just imagine as if the tingling feeling is transferring to that leg. In just a few moments, it will begin to feel numb. This is all quite natural and easy, and you feel very comfortable all the while. You may feel some pressure, but no pain. The memory of the hand falling asleep is being activated in your mind right now.

It is producing the response. Your mind knows how to facilitate these changes. Each time that you practice this, you will find the numbing response is five times faster than the last time. It is five times easier to reproduce, five times quicker, every time that you practice. You are training that part of your mind to interact with you and bring this phenomenon forth. It is quite natural, quite comfortable, and quite easy for you.

LOCAL ANESTHESIA (C)

Induction of choice .... Check for somnambulism ... followed by.....

Now as you go deeper and deeper relaxed, and farther and farther on down, you relax all your muscles and concentrate on the sound of my voice. In your mind's eye, I want you to feel your right hand grow cool, numb, or anesthetized. More cool, more numb, or more anesthetized.

More cool, more numb, or more anesthetized. More cool, or more numb, or more anesthetized.

It feels like a block of ice, or block of wood or as if it is filled with Xylocaine. It begins to feel like a block of ice, or a block of wood, or filled with Xylocaine.

Now I'm going to count slowly from one to five. With each number that passes, your hand becomes number or cooler. When I reach the number five your hand will definitely feel numb.

ONE . . . more cool or numb. TWO . . . more numb or cool. THREE . . . more numb or cool. Your hand should definitely begin to feel cool or numb or anesthetized now. I can even see your right hand becoming paler and it appears to be getting quite cool or numb or anesthetized now. FOUR . . . more cool or numb or anesthetized. . . and FIVE . . . your hand is now cool or numb or anesthetized.

Now let your right hand drift upwards to the area of pain or discomfort. Slowly . . . (pause) . . . now press your hand firmly against the area and transfer all that cool, numb or anesthetic feeling from your hand to the painful or uncomfortable area. Transfer . . . transfer . . . transfer . . . that's it, transfer all that cool or numb or anesthetic feeling to that painful or uncomfortable area.

And when all that cool or numb or anesthetic feeling is transferred to that area, let your hand again drift down to your lap again and relax completely, going into a deeper and deeper relaxed state of hypnosis.

I'll now give you a few moments of silence to accomplish all this. That period of silence begins now.

- Embed a subliminal suggestion to facilitate numbness/freezing in the dentist's office..... EMERGE

BRUXISM SCRIPT 1 (C)

Induction of choice .... Check for somnambulism ... followed by.....

Stressful situations occur every day, which may cause us to grit our teeth. Whenever one of these anxiety-producing events happens, or is going to happen, such as ...(insert typical problem)... you unconsciously grit your teeth. Now you have a way of handling the situation, by keeping just enough nervous energy to deal with the task perfectly – and letting go of excess tension. When you're ready to go to sleep at night you can practice, saying something like `Nothing is important enough in life to grind me down.'

Most teeth grinding happens during the night. The cause is that the subconscious mind remembers the stressful or anxiety producing situations which have occurred during the day, or threaten to occur in the future, and replays them many times during the night. Now during the night, the abnormal touch of your teeth will waken you – you'll smile – realize that your subconscious is protecting you, turn over, and go right back to sleep, losing no sleep at all. It's so nice when you're feeling tired to just rest your head and drift down into a nice, deep, comfortable physiological sleep, and so delightful to be aware of that comfortable feeling that you experience when there is an appropriate amount of space between your teeth – no contact.

And whenever you drift down into a nice, deep, comfortable physiological sleep, there is the possibility that on this night or perhaps on the next night, or that this week or the next week, you might grind your teeth.

But from now on, whenever that does occur you will immediately awaken and relax your jaw, before drifting back into that nice, deep, comfortable, physical sleep.

"You know, it's a very nice thing to have a good grip of the hand, and people are often so lazy about exercising - they always find a reason not to. Now, every time you do find yourself starting to grind your teeth, you chose to exercise your grip instead. You get a really, good grip. It's so good to have a nice strong grasp of things. Your unconscious mind knows exactly what I mean and fully grasps everything that it finds gripping."

It's also good to let go and relax – and relaxation is something that now comes naturally to you. Letting go of tension is as easy as can be and each time you feel and experience that sense of `letting go' you go deeper into that lovely calm, relaxing feeling. ....*EMERGE*

BRUXISM SCRIPT 2 (C)

Induction of choice …. Check for somnambulism … followed by…..

…Feeling good about yourself now, release all feelings of guilt or aggression. Things don't bother you like they did in the past. Things that used to upset you or make you nervous, hurt your feelings, embarrass you, or make you angry, no longer have such a profound effect on you. You can now see them more clearly for what they are, and not allow them to upset you.

Anytime you clench or grind your teeth, you become aware on a conscious or subconscious level of what you are doing. ……… As the awareness occurs, you automatically relax every muscle in your body.

Clenching or grinding your teeth is an aggressive or nervous outlet. Instead of grinding your teeth, you now can take a deep breath and completely release the tension. Take a deep breath right now and notice how relaxed you become when you exhale. ….*EMERGE*

BRUXISM SCRIPT 3 (C)

Induction of choice …. Check for somnambulism … followed by…..

When people grind their teeth at night, it occurs for two reasons. First, you store your tension there in your jaw and, secondly, it has become a habit. Let's take the tension out of your jaw and release the pressure. Let's implant that you will do a dental exercise where we replace the habit with a new, better, healthier one that releases the tension. ….. Together we can create this new pattern for health at the same time.

All you have to do is place your attention or consciousness in your jaw. Focus your awareness on your jaw, and notice how tense the muscles are there. The easiest way to release muscle tension is by tightening it, then releasing it. You must do this every night prior to your going to sleep. Clench your teeth firmly together and hold them still for a count of 3...then release and relax the muscles. Do this exercise with me now, clench your teeth firmly, then release. Notice how the muscle is responding.

If it feels warm, that is the blood flowing in it…taking all the tension…all the stress that has chemically built up in your jaw. At night you will do this for two sets of ten times...

When you have released the stress in your jaw there is no need for you to grind or gnash your teeth at night. All that stress is gone. All the tension is taken away. You will have a much more relaxed sleep than you have encountered for a long, long time. In the morning you will feel better rested, knowing you freed yourself from tension prior to sleeping. This is your new habit for health.

You feel so much better now that you handle your stress in a positive way. You no longer have any urge, need, or desire to continue the old destructive pattern. It is just simply a better, more comfortable way of living.

Having just become aware of the pattern helps you to transcend it. You now have the idea that you can recreate your life and learn new methods for handling stress. This leads you to smile.

Imagine right now that you are in the dental office and your dentist is congratulating you on how you have improved. He can physically show you how much more healthy you are now. He is pleased for your success and delighted to see the improvement. ....*EMERGE*

DENTAL PATIENT ANXIETY (C)

Induction of choice .... Check for somnambulism ... followed by.....

Take a deep breath and relax all over. Starting today, beginning right now, we will transfer this feeling of deep relaxation and comfort to your experiences in a dental office.

Your mind has the capacity to stimulate certain chemicals in your brain. One of those chemicals that the brain produces is the endorphin. Endorphins are a group of proteins with potent analgesic properties that occur naturally in the brain. They have been documented as being many times more powerful than morphine. Your mind has the ability to produce them. When the mind releases these proteins, the person experiences a calm, euphoric response. That is, a response where you are in complete calm and relaxation, even a bit giddy with delight.

Let's practice now, and you easily can use this the next time you visit your dentist. It will eliminate all sense of abnormal fear or stress you used to feel there. So, take a deep breath and feel a warm rush of relaxation flow from your brain throughout your body. Just say to yourself, "endorphins, endorphins, endorphins" and your mind will relax, your body will relax.

You see yourself in a calm, pleasant state of mind. The dental procedures will be conducted efficiently and quickly. The time in the chair will seem to go quickly because you are now engaging the euphoric response while you relax in the dental chair.

At all times you will be able to engage in a coherent conversation, follow instructions and feel totally calm and comfortable. Remember the old axiom "anything the mind can conceive the body can achieve."

We are now embedding these ideas firmly into your subconscious mind so that you can envision a comfortable dental visit. The past does not equal the future. Your past negative experiences and fears are now drifting away and being replaced by these positive healthy suggestions. They now embed themselves into your subconscious mind, melting away any fears like distant memories. Now, replacing them with this positive technique and image of your next dental visit...

Practice this daily for the next 21 days and you will be in complete comfort and control the next office visit you have. ....*EMERGE*

PRE-SURGERY WELLNESS (C)

In this heightened state of awareness your subconscious mind is ready and eager to receive the suggestions that you are about to hear. And, you've had your dental surgery and everything went exactly as it should have done. You survived the surgery and now your body and mind need time to recover and heal - for what seemed like an intrusion to you was something your dentist does almost every day of his working life.

Of course you already know that you're in the most capable hands possible because your dentist and his/her team are experts in their field. They have undergone years of training of a most rigorous type and performed countless operations successfully on other patients who are now completely recovered and leading a normal, healthy and happy life - far better than they ever thought possible to lead.

And it's because you trust in them - just as you trust the sound of my voice - that you fully accept and you are happy about everything that has happened to you in your surgery. And in a few days/weeks *(depending upon the nature of the operation)* you'll be well on your way to a full road to recovery and wonder why you ever felt apprehensive about any of this. You may have concerns about your stitches/staples *(depending which your client had)*. This is perfectly normal - your internal organs are now working just as they should - and the gum, teeth, skin and mucus membrane will soon heal as they fuse together again - so that in just a few months scarring will change from red to pink to white - and after a while you will hardly even notice it there.

So settle yourself down even more deeply into your chair and just listen to the sound of my voice. It doesn't matter if you don't concentrate on the words that I speak because your inner mind is absorbing - like a sponge - everything that is said to you during this time.

And although you begin to feel sleepy and so comfortable, you can also let your mind wander and explore the wonderful images that flow into your imagination. ...and dream - a very special dream. You are about to embark on a journey of discovery to a magical, mystical place - a place that is alive with vibrant colors and harmonious sounds - and it's almost as though you're totally detached from your body at this time -

although you know that you can return whenever you wish to check on the progress being made.

So come with me now - along a mountain path that leads to your perfect place. Be aware that as you take each little step - you feel more as though you are floating - just floating along - and you are not alone - you can hear the sound of my voice all the time - and even - perhaps find yourself floating with the person you love the most - enjoying together the wonderful experience that awaits you.

And... the scenery up here is breathtakingly beautiful. The mountains seem to whisper the sounds of love, abundant with life - different shades of green - breathing in harmony with their surroundings. There are trees and rock formations - small clusters of forest - and just a little way down the mountain track that you're standing on, a gently trickling stream, glittering in the sunlight, with another narrow pathway running alongside it.

It's a beautiful day and you know that it's going to be better and brighter than ever before. You can now feel the warmth from the sun on your body and it seems as though it is penetrating every nerve - every cell - every fiber - every consciousness of your being - is totally and completely relaxed - and at peace.

Your mind and body are working in harmony together and in harmony with all creation. The very rays of the sunlight appear to be filled with their healing love - and you can feel this healing being transferred to your body - and your mind - as you drift deeper and deeper into this warm and comfortable relaxing feeling.

...And in your dream, you can dream of how it will be - very soon - to have a healthy mouth... and gums and tongue healthy again - functioning normally - as you know that you're going to do - when you arouse from this beautiful sleep - you will fully accept that time is the greatest healer of all.

See yourself in the future, carrying out ordinary, everyday tasks, with a completely new attitude of mind...because now, you appreciate every aspect of life. You have energy, vitality, positive thoughts and positive feelings. Even the previously most mundane of jobs can seem pleasurable to you - as you focus your mind on whatever you do - and you do - feel so good - wonderfully calm and relaxed and at peace - like you never imagined it possible to be - but you are - alive - and happy - and making the most of each moment of your wonderful life.

You can feel really comfortable now, as you dream your dreams, and see these scenes, and feel the feeling of receiving healing and health and vitality. And your body is breathing - the air that it needs - the prana - the energy - the life force - that is entering your body and filling your lungs - that are working efficiently - just as they always do - extracting the purity of the oxygen that is carried around the bloodstream to soothe and to heal every cell of your mouth and body.

All organs, cells and systems of your body are working in harmony now. Your entire metabolism is becoming finely tuned to your individual needs. Your entire digestive system, from mouth to stomach to elimination, uses the food that you eat more effectively and you limit the quantities of food so that you are eating just the right amount of healthy, nutritious food that you require to give you proper nutrition. You desire only the foods that are consistent and good for you. You feel a sense of acceptance, a feeling of peace and serenity deep within you. You metabolism, during your resting periods, becomes much more natural and is adjusted for your relaxed state

And your entire nervous system begins to function more efficiently and effectively as your automatic nervous system, which controls your heart rate and your breathing without you even needing to be conscious of it doing so, is working in peace and harmony together.

Because of your improved nervous system, your digestion and kidneys begin to function more effectively and you feel a tremendous improvement to your entire being. The blood supply to your vital organs such as your liver, your pancreas and your spleen will nourish these organs more effectively as all the chemistry in your body becomes more balanced and stable.

Your brain waves are becoming balanced and this indicates a more peaceful and restful nature and because of this you are sleeping more soundly and experiencing beautiful dreams. And, when you wake up, you do so with a refreshed and invigorating feeling with full alertness.

And because of your improved biochemical and metabolic system, your general resistance to infections and diseases improves and your blood pressure is normal and you go about your day-to-day activities with a calm serenity.

 Your mind and your body experience healing and health in a natural way - as you look around at the beauty in nature - you appreciate the improved quality of your life - and you feel as though you really are walking on air - happier and healthier than ever before.

And as you leisurely move along the mountain, you look back and see how far you've traveled, surprised at the distance between now and then. Such an immense improvement - but wasn't it only a short while ago - that you went into that theatre (Operating Room) to have yourself healed - and the lights that shone down - on the medical team - made them appear to you - like angels - sent from heaven - to help you - in your time of need.

And your trust in that team was strengthened by the love that you felt - and the desire that you had - to recover - and regain - your rightful state of health - and vitality. And your mind was so calm - just as it is now - for you knew that higher powers - are working for you - as they do.

And you immerse yourself into a gentle hypnotic rest - on the journey - the magical, mystical journey into the mountains where you now find yourself - ready to awaken after your rest - fully recovered and healed.

There is a door on the mountainside - a white door overgrown with moss and hanging leaves but it can open whenever you wish - into a beautiful cavern - somewhat like Aladdin's cave - but even more magical than that. With crystals and jade and sapphires and smoky quartz and other precious stones and minerals hanging from the ceiling and the walls of the cavern.- there is a beautiful blue light that reflects and shimmers and sparkles - alive with energy and love. And when you are ready to venture forward in there you will experience a certain oneness with all of creation - all knowledge.

And as my voice fades - you can allow yourself to explore - and even the sounds of nurses or doctors or other hospital staff - will come to you from a distance. And you can comply with the requests that are beneficial for your future wellbeing - and return - whenever you wish - to the cavern on the hillside - and go deeper and deeper than ever before.

My voice is fading now - just as the memory of that operation is becoming more and more distant. And you find that each hour of each day you begin to feel better and healthier and calmer   You return to this gentle hypnotic rest whenever you like - allowing your body to fully recover - perhaps a few hours - or days - who knows - not so long - for in hypnosis time changes - just as it does in your dreams.

So have a beautiful dream and enjoy these relaxing feelings – while your body feels the healing that it is receiving - and when you're ready to return to the here and now - come back gently and open your eyes and take a nice deep breath - and just trust in the healing that's taking place from within.

(Allow your client to remain in hypnosis for a few minutes before counting them out - Relaxed and refreshed - mind and body returning to healthy functioning awareness).

FEAR OF INJECTIONS (C)

Induction of choice …. Check for somnambulism … followed by…..

Now as you lie comfortably there with your eyes closed - comfortable and aware that you are here because you want to learn to use your own subconscious abilities to help you to eliminate the anxiety you experience when you visit the doctor's for an injection.

And so, as you begin to relax and to drift down into trance - deeper now - into a deep trance state - I want you to take your time - not go too quickly - yet - because there are some things that you need to first understand – so please listen carefully now.

First, you need to understand that you already have the ability to lose an arm - or a hand – that is, to become totally unaware of just where that arm is positioned - or the fingers - and you do have an ability to be unconcerned about exactly where the feelings for that ear or thumb went.

You do have an ability - a subconscious ability - you can learn to use - an ability to turn off the sensation in an arm - a leg - or even your face - your jaw - your gum - in fact - any place.

And once you discover how it feels to feel nothing at all - whenever you want or need that to occur - then you can create a comfortable numb feeling any time - anywhere that is useful for you.

And I don't know if your unconscious mind can allow you to discover that numb feeling in the right hand or a finger of the left hand first - a tiny area of numbness - a comfortable, tickly feeling - a heavy - enveloping numbness – that seems to spread within time - over the back of the hand - covering that hand – or any part of you that you direct your attention to - it just fades away - but you don't know how it feels to feel that something that is not there - so I would like you to just reach over to that numb, comfortable area - that numb, comfortable hand – now touch it - and feel that touching - as you begin to pinch yourself there - a sensation that you may be aware of at first - but as you continue to pinch yourself - something special happens here –

You begin to experience and discover that there are times when you feel nothing at all there - that sensation just seems to fade away - as you learn how to allow your subconscious mind to do that for you - to turn off those sensations and as that ability grows and you become more aware - that you really do know how - to really turn off that part - really know how to switch off those sensations and allow any feelings in that hand to just disappear from that hand - or from anywhere - your other hand can return to its resting position - and you can drift up towards the surface of wakeful awareness - so go ahead now - as you relax –

Re-experience that numbness more and more clearly - and so you can drift up - and then back down - as you learn even more about your own ability - in your own time - in your own way - you can practice this self-learning - this ability to do that for you at any time - at any place.

Now, with your eyes closed, you can relax more deeply than before – aware of that new learning. That new ability to switch off that discomfort. You can visualize now as vividly as you can - see yourself at your next visit to the doctor's office - and notice how calm you are feeling as you stand at the receptionist's desk - in plenty of time for your appointment.

You are now sit in the waiting area - feeling calm and unconcerned - confident in your ability to control the sensations - you smile at the others who are waiting with you - pleased to be able to allow your own calm and confident manner to soothe the minds of others - as they wait too be called.

As you sit there, you practice again your ability to turn off the sensations there - and experience that numbness - as the sensation in the arm fades – that numbness spreading - that woolly, thick feeling of no feeling at all - and you relax experiencing a total, inner calm.

When your turn comes to be called into the surgery (doctor's office) - you take a long, deep breath - and as you expel all the air from your lungs - you breathe out anxiety - fear - and then breathe in - calm – confident. As you sit in the chair, you will experience a comfortable sensation as calm fills your mind - as you relax - concentrating now on that switch that will allow you to experience that sensation of no sensation - as your doctor/dentist (or nurse) gently and carefully carries out the work that needs to be done.

And when you roll up your sleeve - ready for the injection - you will be calm and comfortable. But, I really don't want you to giggle when you experience that tickle - and I don't want you to drift off too deeply into a trance too quickly - as the numbness begins to develop. You will be pleasurably surprised at how calm and relaxed you will become, as your doctor, appreciating your necessary co-operation - completes his work easily – skillfully. You will enjoy being the person who relaxes there in that chair - and allows your subconscious to use that special ability that you have learned.

You are no longer bothered or concerned, as you now take control of that fear - and unlearn that fear - seeing it now for exactly what it was. No more imagining in that way that tells you that there are things to fear here - as your subconscious mind takes care of you. And, it doesn't really matter exactly how you tell your subconscious mind what to do or how your subconscious mind does it for you, the only thing of importance is that you know that you can lose those sensations - the discomfort - just as easily as opening your eyes. And while you drift in your mind and then return when it's time - back to wakeful awareness - quite completely now.   … EMERGE

PROMOTE HEALING BEFORE SURGERY (C)

Induction of choice …. Check for somnambulism … followed by…..

Take a nice long slow deep breath in and slowly breathe out. . . We will take three of these breaths. Notice that on each one you feel more and more relaxed. Now once again take a long slow, slow deep breath in - and out...Notice how you are beginning to relax. Take another slow deep breath in...and out...Notice how much more relaxed you are.

Again, a long slow, slow deep breath and this time when you exhale, your eyes close naturally, as you relax deeply. Notice how much more relaxed you are. Continue to breathe normally and naturally. Let each and every breath you take, relax you more and more... Allow yourself to begin to go into dream time...

The sound of my voice is relaxing, and relaxing is a pleasure as you drift deeper and deeper into dream time. To help you go even deeper into this quiet relaxed state, we will descend a staircase of relaxation.

Imagine yourself standing on the top of the staircase of relaxation, wearing a loose fitting garment, made of a very fine fabric; it is your favorite color. What color might that be today?...

As you descend, you find yourself sinking deeper and deeper into the chair or bed that you are resting on, feeling more and more relaxed. With each step, you double your sense of relaxation. As you go through this exercise, you may have a sensation of heaviness, you may have a sensation of floating like a feather, of being light and airy or you may just know that you are deeply relaxed. Whatever you experience is just right for you, you are doing fine.

Begin to descend now. Ten-floating deeper and deeper down,. Nine-deeper, Eight ... letting go of all doubt, worry, anxiety. You don't need that any more. Seven-deeper and deeper relaxed. Six-the longer it takes you to relax, the deeper you go. Five-we will pause here as it is time to call upon your spiritual guide who will be with you on this journey. It may be God, an angel, a saint, or a feeling of a spiritual connection with the creative force.

I will give you a time of silence to make contact with your spiritual partner...(30 seconds). You are doing fine. Step down to four ... relaxing and going deeper. Three-letting go, going deeper. Two- deeper and deeper. One - very deeply relaxed.

Now let yourself travel easily and effortlessly to a lake. Imagine it is summertime, there is a warm breeze, you can hear the waves lapping at the shore as you gaze out over the lake. It is your lake of peace.

The waves have a rhythm. They calm and relax you. Listen as they begin to help you relax your body so that the anesthetic you will be receiving for your surgical procedure is taken easily. In fact, you need only a very small amount of anesthetic, because your body is co-operating so well. It is bending into the procedure.

As a result, very little anesthetic is being used the entire time of the surgical procedure. You are in control of what is happening to your body. You have set the processes into motion through your ability to relax on command, your command. The waves continue in their rhythmic pattern.

Every time you hear the phrase, "You are doing fine," all of your healing systems come together to function in a normal healthy manner. They create complete recovery within and without. Relax and take a deep breath... You are doing fine.

Let yourself sink deeper and deeper into a peaceful relaxed state. Your mind begins to drift. It is like a dream. You begin rehearsing for your surgical procedure. It is safe and enjoyable to be this relaxed. Through the power of your imagination, you see yourself walking into the medical facility. You say to yourself, "This is where I am going to get well. This is where my body is going to be repaired so it can get well....This is where I can go whenever I need to...to help my physician help me towards wellness....I make the decisions for my wellbeing...I have decided that this is a surgical procedure that will bring my body to wellness... The surgeon and staff are here to help me... The word for the day is co-operation...We are a team,... we work together."

As a result of these positive thoughts, you can see, feel and know just how you are entering the medical facility. You walk with confidence, you speak with confidence and you smile with confidence and pride. This is your decision. I'll give you time to rehearse this scene...*(30 seconds)*

Good, you arc doing fine. Notice how good you feel about being in control of your thoughts and feelings. Good, you are doing fine. Each, and every time you practice this, you become calmer and more relaxed... and this is so.

What we picture in the theatre of our mind becomes our reality. You are now your own writer, actor, editor and producer. Medical science has found that a person with a good attitude about the outcome of their surgery has a 100% better chance of recovery than one who has a negative or pessimistic attitude.

You are creating, through mind power, the positive attitude needed to help you to complete recovery. Congratulations! You are doing fine. Now let the scene change to the room where the procedure is to take place. If you do not have a definite picture, make one up. You are feeling relaxed and confident, want that to happen, let it happen. Notice how much more relaxed you are. You are doing fine. This is your decision.

The physician is there to help you repair your body so that you can have wellness and peace of mind. Co-operation is the word for the day. You relax even deeper as the anesthetic is administered, and, you only need a very small amount to get your body ready for the procedure, and this is so. You are doing fine.

Once again, it is you who have made the decision to co-operate and as a result of the relaxation, your body only needs a very small amount of to keep you at the perfect level for the procedure. You can hear noises around you, but you pay no attention to them.

The scene changes... back to the lake. You find yourself on a lovely safe swing. It has a nice steady rhythm and you feel calm and relaxed as you look out onto your lake of peace. Calm and relaxed… Enjoying the scene that is before you; Feeling the rhythm of the swing, smelling the aromas of nature, enjoying the sun on the water and the seagulls sailing through the air. Calm and relaxed...calm and relaxed...calm and relaxed.

Your body co-operates with the skillful hands of the surgeon. It opens up easily, it has only the exact amount of blood flow that is necessary to maintain perfect balance. In fact, your body knows exactly what to do, and it does it in concert with the surgeon. All of your vital signs are in perfect order; blood pressure perfect, heart rate perfect, breathing normal.

You are enjoying your time at the lake, calm and relaxed...calm and relaxed. You are doing fine. Interestingly enough, from the very moment that you decided to have this surgery done, your body began the healing process. Your body knows what to do in order to get you to wellness. All systems are go. The healing system is in gear, the immune system is functioning perfectly, everything about you is co-operating with your medical team. They are your medical team, and you are the captain. They are doing the work that is theirs to do, while your healing system and immune system are doing their work.

All of your blood cells are doing their job perfectly. In fact, this is the easiest surgical procedure that your medical team has ever done. The reason for this is that you are giving the orders to your healing system to co-operate fully with your medical team.

I will give you a few moments to let these suggestions take complete effect upon you...(1 min)

Good you are doing fine.. When it is time,... when the procedure is complete... and not before, you find: The dream is about over, soon you will come to full wakeful consciousness. Notice how relaxed and comfortable you feel. You have an appetite and can eat small amounts of food, easily and effortlessly. You find that you are thirsty and drink water easily. You can void body waste easily. All of your organs are functioning normally and naturally. You feel wonderful, as if you have had a magical summer nap! You are doing fine.

There is an awareness that a procedure has taken place. You can feel a little pressure, but that is all. Any discomfort is minimal and you are full of energy. You are in control and healing has begun and will continue. You are well. It is now time to thank your spiritual partner for being with you on this important journey ... in a moment's silence beginning now.....(15 sec)

The following are positive suggestions that I would like you to repeat mentally after me, it makes them even stronger this way:

- Every day in every way, I am getting better and better.
- I am in control. I create my own reality.
- Negative thoughts have no power over me. I am in control.
- I create my own reality through the power of my mind, and this is so.
- I persistently think and act in the direction of my good and my goal; to be a happy, healthy, relaxed person.
- I am love. I am loving, loved and beloved.
- I am healed by the Creative Force within me.
- My body knows just how to keep me well and I pay close attention to its signals. I obey those signals, I relax, I let go and stay well.
- My body systems are co-operating with the surgical procedure, we are all working together to create healing.
- My blood pressure is normal. My blood count is perfect.
- My lungs breathe easily and effortlessly.
- Every day in every way, I am getting better and better...

When the time is right, just open your eyes feeling wonder-full, knowing that you are in control of all that happens to you. You do create your own reality. Today, your reality is that of a relaxed healthy human being, feeling balanced in body, mind and spirit. ...And, so it is.

When you are using this technique during the surgical procedure, continue to stay at your lake of peace until you hear that it is time to awaken. The recovery room nurse is saying your name. Notice how good you feel and will continue to feel. Your recovery happens quickly, easily and effortlessly, and this is so.

You are doing fine. If you are listening to this in preparation for the procedure, you may open your eyes now, knowing that you have created a new reality for yourself, and this is so.

NOTE: Every time you say, "You are doing fine," insert the person's name. Let your voice be expressive of the wellness that is there for your client. You, through the power of your words, give hope and encouragement to this person. Your voice is what has been there for them during this stressful event. You do make a difference. YOU ARE DOING FINE !!!)

PROMOTE HEALING FOLLOWING DENTAL SURGERY (C)

Choose the induction of your choice and then:

In this heightened state of awareness your subconscious mind is ready and eager to receive the suggestions that you are about to hear. And you've had your (gum surgery) and everything went exactly as it should have done. You survived the surgery well, and now your body, and your mind need time to recover and heal. For what seemed like an intrusion to you, was something your dental surgeon does almost every day of her (his) working life.

Of course you already know that you're in the most capable hands possible because your surgeon and his team are experts in their field. They have undergone years of training of a most rigorous type and performed countless operations successfully on other patients who are now completely recovered and leading a normal, healthy and happy life - far better than they ever thought possible to lead.

And it's because you trust in them - just as you trust the sound of my voice - you fully accept and you're happy about everything that has happened to you in your surgery. And... in a few days/weeks (depending upon the nature of the operation), you'll be well on your way to a full road to recovery and wonder why you ever felt apprehensive about any of this. You may have concerns about your stitches/staples (depending which your client had)… this is perfectly normal - your internal organs are now working just as they should - and the skin will soon heal as it fuses together again - so that in just a few months that scarring will change from red to pink to white - and after a while you will hardly even notice it there.

So settle yourself down even more deeply into your chair and just listen to the sound of my voice. It doesn't matter if you don't concentrate on the words that I speak because your inner mind is absorbing - like a sponge - everything that is said to you during this time.

And, although you begin to feel sleepy and so comfortable - you can also let your mind wander and explore the wonderful images that flow into your imagination - and dreamlike - a very special dream - that you are about to embark on a journey of discovery to a magical, mystical place - a place that is alive with vibrant colors and harmonious sounds - and it's almost as though you're totally detached from your body at this time - although you know that you can return whenever you wish to check on the progress being made.

So come with me now - along a beautiful path that leads to your perfect place. Be aware that as you take each little step - you feel more as though you are floating - just floating along - and you're not alone. You can hear the sound of my voice all the time - and even - perhaps find yourself floating with the person you love the most - enjoying together the wonderful experience that awaits you.

And, the scenery up here is breathtakingly beautiful - the hills around seem to whisper the sounds of love - abundant with life - different shades of green - breathing in harmony with their surroundings - there are trees and rock formations - small clusters of forest - and just a little way down the country track that you're walking on, a gently trickling stream, glittering in the sunlight, with another narrow pathway running alongside it.

It's a beautiful day and you know that it's going to be better and brighter than ever before. You can now feel the warmth from the sun on your body and it seems as though it is penetrating every nerve - every cell - every fiber - every consciousness of your being - is totally and completely relaxed - and at peace.

Your mind and body are working in harmony together and in harmony with all creation. The very rays of the sunlight appear to be filled with their healing love - and you can feel this healing being transferred to your body - and your mind - as you drift deeper and deeper into this warm and comfortable relaxing feeling.

And, in your dream you can dream of how it will be - very soon - to be healthy again - functioning normally - as you know that you're going to do - when you arouse from this beautiful sleep - you will fully accept that time is the greatest healer of all.

See yourself in the future, - carrying out ordinary, everyday tasks, with a completely new attitude of mind - because now you appreciate every aspect of life - you have energy - vitality - positive thoughts and positive feelings - and even the previously most mundane of jobs can seem pleasurable to you - as you focus your mind on whatever you do - and you do - feel so good - wonderfully calm and relaxed and at peace - like you never imagined it possible to be - but you are alive - and happy - and making the most of each moment of your wonderful life.

You can feel really comfortable now, as you dream your dreams - and see these scenes - and feel the feeling of receiving healing and health and vitality - and your body is breathing - the air that it needs - the prana - the energy - the life force - that is entering your body and filling your lungs - that are working efficiently - just as they always do - extracting the purity of the oxygen that is carried around the bloodstream to soothe and to heal every cell of your body.

All organs and cells and systems of your body are working in harmony now. Your whole metabolism is becoming finely tuned to your individual needs. Your mouth and entire digestive system uses the food that you eat more effectively and you limit the quantities of food so that you're eating just the right amount of healthy, nutritious food that you require to give you proper nutrition. You desire only the foods that are good for you. You feel a sense of acceptance, a feeling of peace and serenity deep within you. You metabolism during your resting periods becomes much more natural and is adjusted for your relaxed state

And your entire nervous system begins to function more efficiently and effectively as your automatic nervous system, which controls your heart rate and your breathing without you even needing to be conscious of it doing so, is working in peace and harmony together.

Because of your improved nervous system, your digestion and kidneys begin to function more effectively and you feel a tremendous improvement to your entire being. The blood supply to your vital organs such as your liver, your pancreas and your spleen will nourish these organs more effectively as all the chemistry in your body becomes more balanced and stable.

Your brain waves are becoming balanced and this indicates a more peaceful and restful nature and because of this you're sleeping more soundly and experiencing beautiful dreams. And when you wake up, you do so with a refreshed and invigorating feeling with full alertness.

And because of your improved biochemical and metabolic system, your general resistance to infections and diseases improves and your blood pressure is normal and you go about your day-to-day activities with a calm serenity.

Your mind and your body experience healing and health in a natural way. As you look around at the beauty in nature, you appreciate the improved quality of your life. And you feel as though you really are walking on air, happier and healthier than ever before.

And as you leisurely move through the countryside along the mountain, you look back and see how far you've traveled- Surprised at the distance...between now and then. Such an immense improvement. But, wasn't it only a short while ago that you went into that dental office to have yourself healed. And the lights that shone down, on the medical team, made them appear to you like angels sent from Heaven to help you in your time of need.

And your trust in that team was strengthened by the love that you felt. And the desire that you had to recover, and regain your rightful state of health, and vitality. And your mind was so calm, just as it is now, for you knew that higher powers are working for you, as they do.

And you immerse yourself into a gentle hypnotic rest on the journey. The magical, mystical journey into the mountains, where you now find yourself ready to awaken after your rest. Fully recovered and healed.

There is a door on the mountainside. A white door, overgrown with moss and hanging leaves but it can open whenever you wish, into a beautiful cavern, somewhat like Aladdin's cave. But even more magical than that, with crystals and jade and sapphires and smoky quartz and other precious stones and minerals hanging from the ceiling and the walls of the cavern. There is a beautiful blue light that reflects and shimmers and sparkles, alive with energy and love, and when you are ready to venture forward in there you will experience a certain oneness with all of creation, all knowledge.

And as my voice fades, you can allow yourself to explore, and even the sounds of nurses or doctors or other hospital staff, will come to you from a distance. And you can comply with the requests that are beneficial for your future wellbeing, and return, whenever you wish, to the cavern on the hillside, and go deeper and deeper than ever before.

My voice is fading now, just as the memory of that surgery is becoming more and more distant. And you find that each hour of each day you begin to feel better and healthier and calmer   You return to this gentle hypnotic rest whenever you like, allowing your body to fully recover. Perhaps a few hours, or days, who knows. Not so long, for in hypnosis time changes, just as it does in your dreams.

So have a beautiful dream and enjoy these relaxing feelings. While your body feels the healing that it is receiving. And... when you're ready to return to the here and now, come back gently and open your eyes and take a nice deep breath. And just trust in the healing that's taking place from within.

(Allow your client to remain in hypnosis for a few minutes before counting them out).

One - two - three - eyelids beginning to flicker - four - coming slowly back and five - eyes open - wide awake. Relaxed and refreshed - mind and body returning to healthy functioning awareness.

SCRIPT: IDEO-MOTOR FINGER RESPONSE FOR THERAPY (C)

NOTE : This is an efficient way to work with clients who achieve deep states easily. You can have your client use finger signals to let you know when she has arrived. And later to give you information direct from the subconscious mind.

Induction of choice .... Check for somnambulism ... followed by.....

You may allow yourself to be relaxed and at ease now, and you can continue to feel calm, relaxed and peaceful as I talk to you. You are beginning to experience the wonderful sensations that relaxation brings to you. . . relaxed and comfortable. In fact, you can allow yourself to become more relaxed with each breath you take, listening to the sound of my voice. With each sound that you hear, you become more and more relaxed. You become more relaxed as you are experiencing wonderful peace of mind.

There are some questions, which I would like to ask you. Now, these questions can be answered "yes" or "no"....Unless I feel it is important to discuss an area with you to remove any blocks to your subconscious. This will be done only with your consent.

I am going to ask you some questions which can be answered either "yes" or "no". Your subconscious mind is able to answer each question I ask you. You may take a mental journey and let your subconscious respond to the questions.

Your subconscious mind is controlling the fingers of your hand. I request that your subconscious mind pick out a "yes" finger, and that finger is becoming very light. In fact, it is lighter than air and just wants to float up. Don't resist it, don't assist it, just let it drift up. The "yes" finger is beginning to rise. That's good. Your _____finger of your_____ - hand is the "yes" finger.

Now just let your finger float back down, and as it does, you become twice as relaxed.

Now, allow your subconscious mind to pick out a "no" finger. Now, just let the "no" finger begin to rise. Your subconscious mind is causing your "no" finger to rise. That's good. Your _____finger of your _____ hand is the "no" finger. Now, just let your finger float back down, and as it does, you become twice as relaxed.

Your subconscious mind is controlling your "yes" finger and your "no" finger. Let us begin with the questions and just let your subconscious answer "yes" or "no".

1. Is there some emotional reason that makes you _____ ?
2. Have you gone through some experience in the past that is causing _____?
3. Are you identifying with someone else, perhaps a parent or other significant other who _____?
4. Are you using _____ to punish yourself?
5. Are you using _____ to punish someone else?
6. Are you trying to harm yourself _____ ?
7. Is there any conflict concerning sex that contributes to _____?

8. Are you _____ because you feel guilty about something?
9. Do you _____ when you feel lonely?
10. Do you _____ when you feel stress or tension?
11. Do you _____ when you are angry?
12. Do you _____ to pamper or appease yourself?
13. Do you _____ as a means of drawing attention toward yourself?

14. Is there any subconscious reason you need to continue _____?
    (If "yes" ask, "can you, or do you want to discuss why you need to continue?")

15. Is it O.K. with your subconscious mind to get rid of _____?
    (If answer is "no" ask, "Can you, or do you want to discuss why you do not want to be rid of ------?")

Go to Forgiveness, Regression, or Somatic Bridge, etc. EMERGE

EMERGING YOUR CLIENT/PATIENT (D)

Many practitioners take advantage of this entrainment window to re-emphasize how well the procedure went, and how rapidly they'll heal with a minimum of discomfort, etc.

"Now, I'm going to count up from one to five, and then I'll say, "Fully aware." When I say the number five, your eyes will open and you'll be fully aware, feeling calm, rested, refreshed, and relaxed.

Alright. One - slowly, calmly, easily, you're returning to your full awareness once again, secure in the knowledge that the procedure went very well, and that you will heal quickly and comfortably.

Two - each muscle and nerve in your body is loose and limp and relaxed, and you feel wonderfully good in every way. And each time you visit the dentist you go deeper relaxed each time deeper.

Three - from head to toe, you are feeling perfect in every way. Physically perfect… mentally perfect… emotionally calm and serene.

Four - your eyes begin to feel sparkling clear under your eyelids, and on the next number I count, your eyelids will open, you'll be fully aware, feeling calm, rested, refreshed, relaxed, invigorated, full of energy, and perhaps even slightly hungry *(a patient cannot feel nauseous and hungry at the same time.)*

Number Five, number five *(with authority)* … open your eyes, open your eyes *(practitioner could gently snap their fingers at this point as an audible, external anchor to the patient)* - you're fully aware now. Eyes open. Fully aware… Fully aware…. Take a good, deep breath.. fill up your lungs and stretch, feeling absolutely wonderful in every way."

NOTE *that your patient is still slightly in-state for the first two or three minutes after opening their eyes following a session, and are still accepting of positive suggestions (and equally susceptible to negative ones).*

NOTE: *Your patient should be able to respond to normal conversation at this point. If you detect any confusion or hesitation in their responses, they could still be enjoying an entrained state, in which case you can ask them to close their eyes again and give them a 3 count, with your voice becoming more authoritative as you reach the number three.*

EMERGING WITH POST HYPNOTIC SUGGESTION FOR FAST HYPNOSIS (D)

In a few moments…when I count up to '*seven*"…you will open your eyes….and be wide awake again…. You will wake up feeling wonderfully better for this long sleep. … You will wake up feeling completely relaxed……mentally and physically….feeling quite calm and composed.

From now on…..you will never have to wait to go into this wonderful state of hypnosis again. … From now on….*whenever you want me to give you treatment*….all I shall have to do is ask you to lie back comfortably….and listen to my voice. … While you are listening to the sound of my voice….I shall say: *Go to sleep!*

And from now on….whenever you hear me say……'*Go to sleep'* your eyes will always close immediately…..and you will always fall immediately into a sleep….just as deep as this one. It doesn't matter whether it is *tomorrow…..next week….next month*….or even *next year.*

From now on….whenever you hear me say….'*Go to sleep'*……Your eyes will always close immediately…..and you will always fall immediately into a sleep….just as deep as this one. And that is exactly what is going to happen when you come to see me next.

After our preliminary chat…..as soon as you are ready for treatment…. I shall ask you to lay back comfortably in the chair….and look straight at me. While you are looking at me….I shall say: *Go to sleep!*

And next time……and, indeed, on every future occasion when you want me to give you treatment….the moment you hear me say….'Go to sleep"…your eyes will close immediately….and you will fall immediately into a sleep….just as deep as this one.

In a few moments…when I count up to '*seven*"…you will open your eyes….and be wide awake again. You will wake up feeling wonderfully better for this long sleep.

You will wake up feeling completely relaxed, mentally and physically, feeling quite calm and composed. One ....two ....three ....four ....five.....six....seven!   Open your eyes.

GREY ROOM TECHNIQUE FOR GENERAL WELL-BEING (C)

There is a room that exists deep in your own subconscious mind. It is room that you created _____ years ago (when you began worrying, feeling anxious). Now what makes this room so unusual is the round grey walls and dome-like ceiling. Very much the way an igloo might appear inside. Inside this room you can find all your emotional ties, mental ties and physical ties to (the worrying habit). Inside this room you can also find all your connections to worrying activities in your life. Whether at home, or at work, on the road, or at social events.

And because this is your room, deep in your subconscious mind. You know it only exists because you created it __ years ago. And you know when all your emotional ties, mental ties and physical ties to worrying and all your smoking connections to activities in your life are broken completely and permanently that room will close down. Completely shrink away into nothingness. .. and be gone. Because it will no longer serve a purpose.

Now, (name) remaining comfortable, well, safe, deeply relaxed and hypnotized, with our relaxation, sleep and hypnosis growing constantly deeper and more complete, simply find yourself in this comfortable, small and very pleasant grey-walled room. You are totally free of any claustrophobic feelings..... you just feel welcome, right at home, here. This room is small round, grey-walled and it has a domed ceiling... the way an igloo might be inside. And you now sense that this grey-walled room is actually your own subconscious mind...the core of your being... the very center of you.

You now notice that, clinging to the walls of this room...all over... are bits of what appear to be paper! Some are red; and some are white............Moving close to the wall, of this room... all over ... on little bits of what appear to be red paper are all the negative thought and emotional energies and feelings from your past. Like fear, doubt, guilt, hatred, anxiety, rejection, and unhappiness! All the negative, depressing, inhibiting, defeating, thought and emotional energies and feelings from your past are stored in this room of your subconscious, on these little red bits of what appear to be paper.

Now. Become aware of this! You can pull these red bits of what appear to be paper down from the walls. You can crumple them in your hands until your hands are full, and you can take them over to where a hole about eight inches in diameter has opened in the center of the floor, and

pour them through that hole and watch them dissipate, disappear, disintegrate into nothingness! So that these can never get back again! You can sense that, with four or five trips, gathering down handfuls and carrying them to the hole and pouring them through, you can clean all of the negative and emotional energies from your inner self. So, now, at the count of one, I want you to start working at it. I will sit quietly and wait until you are finished. When you are through, just let me know by extending the index finger of your right hand until I say thank you."
…………….. ………...Now start at the count of one, and clean it up! Three …two … one!

Be patient and wait! With some client's . this will take four or five full minutes. If you see obvious signs of struggle or distress, simply ask,

"What's going on?"

(You will probably get a reply similar to this): *"It won't come down!"*

Hypnotist: *"What won't come down? …..Which one?"*

Client: *"Hate!"* (Or guilt or fear, etc.)

Hypnotist: *"All right, get hold of it. At the count of one, its resistance will fade, and with a little pull, it will almost fall off in your hand!" "Three…two…one!"* Snap fingers, not too loudly.

At this point, if the client still shows signs of struggle or seems still unable to get the piece to come loose, simply suggest that he remember any that he doesn't get, but leave them and go on to the others and give you the signal when he has finished getting rid of all that he can. Explain that he feels free of any fear of any which he has to leave, because he knows that he can deal with those later.

Now (name), notice that the white bits… the good, positive energizing, helpful thought and emotional energies and feelings are expanding… growing to fill all the space left by the red ones you disposed of… growing, expanding!… until they fill the whole walls and ceiling with beautiful, wonderful, positive, white! Feel the resurgence of positive energy, now, within yourself, as you notice that the hole in the floor has closed itself and the entire atmosphere of the room is becoming white! …beautiful, pure, uplifting, energizing white!… Take a deep breath and inhale the purity, the strength, the self confidence, the love, the peace, the assurance, the freedom of this atmosphere! Feel it, permeating every cell and every atom of your being!

"From this moment forward, moment by moment, minute by minute, hour by hour, day by day, the thought and emotional energies of your subconscious remain so positive, so calm, so stable… like now, that every part of you…body and mind… remains calm, objective and creative; and functions to absolute perfection… just the way God

designed and made you to function. (make sure this statement is congruent to the client's belief structure)

(Brief Pause) - *"At the count of one, this entire scene will disappear, but the beautiful positive effect will continue. Three...two ...one! The scene disappears and you are beautifully relaxed and hypnotized...resting beautifully... here in my office.*

TEACHING SELF HYPNOSIS
In using this script, it is advisable to see if your client is comfortable with the imagery of an escalator or elevator. Also, are they comfortable with "basement". Knowing their comfort levels with these concepts will avoid having them abreact to it)

Dave Elman Induction followed by:

Following my suggestions, guides you deeper into relaxation. The deeper you go into relaxation the better your feel and the better you feel the more and more your body relaxes with just wonderful feelings going through your body and happy thoughts going through your mind. So relax, and let yourself go. Now I want you to relax still to a deeper state of relaxation. Much more relaxed. So again will count from five down to one and as I count from five down to one, your body will double the relaxation you have right now automatically. 5 ...Relaxation starting to double. 4... Relaxation doubling more and more. 3...Very comfortable very relaxed. 2...Relaxation is now almost doubled in your body. 1...Relaxation now has doubled in your body from every tissue, every organ, every gland, every part of you has doubled in its relaxation. You feel fine.

I want you to imagine, or visualize, that in front of you. there is a long staircase, that is leading down into deeper relaxation. We have never found a basement, a bottom of a person's ability to relax. It's endless. Every breath that you exhale, takes you down another step on this staircase of relaxation.

Every tissue takes you deeper into an endless state of relaxation. You drift down feeling wonderful, feeling comfortable. Relax and just let yourself go. Just relax and let yourself go. I still want you to relax to a much more relaxed state. Already with your light switch in the off position, every muscle becomes dormant, quiet unable to more, but again I will count, but this time from ten down to one. As I count from ten down to one your conscious mind will relax as much as your body is relaxed and your mind and body will double the relaxation that it has at that time on each and every count. 10...Your mind is as relaxed as the body's relaxed and the body is doubling its relaxation. 9... The mind is relaxed as the body is relaxed, and the body is doubling its relaxation again. 8... Mind relaxed as the body is relaxed and the body again is doubling the relaxation it has at this time. 7... The same thing. 6...Keep right on going now.   5...4...3...2...1... Mind relaxed as the body is relaxed and your body has doubled its relaxation many times over.

By relaxation, I mean the absence of all muscle contractions. Your body is loose, limp and motionless. Your muscles offering no resistance just as if you were a rag doll. Complete relaxation means the absence movement. It means the complete absence of holding any part of your body rigid. So, as you are completely relaxed, all the muscles attached to your bones are limp. If you make any voluntary movements you can only do so by contracting some group of muscles, but when you allow these muscles to become completely dormant, your nerves to and from these muscles carry no messages and with your light switch off, the nerves are completely inactive. And it is certain that complete relaxation in any set of nerves simply means zero activity in these nerves. And it is physically impossible for you to be nervous in any part of your body. You're feeling better than you have felt in a long time. Outside noises will not distract you. Any sounds you may hear will only assist you in relaxing more and more deeply and you do go deeper. With every breath, you go down another step on that endless staircase of relaxation. The sound of my voice keeps guiding you deeper into relaxation.

Following my suggestions keeps guiding you into deeper relaxation. And the more and more you allow your body to relax the better you feel and the better you feel the more your mind and body will relax. You have complete control over every nerve in your body, control over your whole nervous system. And, as you have selected to place your light switch in the off position, every nerve in your body becomes quiet, dormant and you drift much deeper, much deeper into relaxation.

And now, there are only three more levels of relaxation for you to go into now. Level A, level B, and level C. Now to accomplish these levels, you must know it will work, let it work. You can feel it working, feel it working as if you are going down an escalator to deeper levels at all times. So now I want you to go from where you are to Level A, thousands of times deeper. You know it will work, let it work. Feel it working, feel yourself sinking down to level A as if you are going down an escalator. Very good. Now I want you to go from level A to level B. Again, you know it will work, let it work. Feel it work as if you are going down an escalator from level A to level B, many times deeper, automatically going down. Very good.

Now I want you to go from level B to level C your basement of relaxation today. You know it will work, let it work. Feel it work. Feel yourself sinking down many times deeper to level C. That's fine.

Now with your light switch in the off position, shutting down the electricity to every muscle in your body, I want you to try to lift your right leg (5 second pause*) stop trying. And let your body go much deeper. Now I want you to try and lift your left leg (5* second pause*) stop trying and let your body still go deeper. Now I want you to try and lift your right arm (5* second pause*) stop trying and let your body still go deeper. All the way down to the very bottom of relaxation where you will be so peaceful, happy and content. Every day you will feel better and better, happier and happier and more contented each time you enter this beautiful state of relaxation. You will go much deeper than the time before.*

"Whenever you enter this state, allow yourself to go back into the same beautiful state that you are now in. Each time allowing yourself to go back deeper, each time enjoying it more and more, feeling terrific in every way. Whenever you enter this state, the instant you close your eyes, you mentally reach up and turn your light switch into the off position, all electricity flowing from your brain to every muscle in your body becomes disconnected. And, your muscles become instantly calm, very deeply relaxed and unable to operate. And the sound of my voice guides you deeper into relaxation.

EMERGE

APPENDIX 1

HYPNOSIS VOCABULARY

ABREACTION: "Abnormal Reaction - Emotional purging by taking out or acting out repressed, or partially repressed, harmful material. Reliving a moment all over again.

AGE REGRESSION: The phenomenon of returning in one's mind, as well as in one's behavior, to some earlier subsequent period, e.g. first birthday.

AMNESIA: Loss of ability to recall conscious past experiences. It may cover a large field of memories or be confined to specific episodes. Suggestions of Hypnosis are often helpful in removing it temporarily and, occasionally, permanently.

AMNESIA, POST-HYPNOTIC: Loss of memory for happenings occurring during hypnosis, or selectively, for whatever the hypnotist suggested for them to forget.

AMNESIA, LOCALIZED: Loss of memory with regard to an incident, experience, place or time.

AMNESIA, SPONTANEOUS: A form of amnesia occurring in a subject without receiving any suggestion to this effect. Spontaneous amnesia is a simple psychological defense mechanism.

ANIMAL MAGNETISM: Mesmer's name for hypnotism selected on the assumption that the state is related to the phenomenon of ordinary magnetism.

ARM LEVITATION: A technique of raising a client's arm by giving suggestions of weightlessness. Used for inductions.

AUTO – HYPNOSIS: Auto-hypnosis is a kind of verbal conditioning. In this procedure, person develops into a good CLIENT, and thoroughly trained in proper instructions is allowed to carry on by himself. (**Self-hypnosis**)

AUTOMATIC NERVOUS SYSTEM: is a vast involuntary system of widely distributed nerve fibers which innervate smooth muscles and glands. The automatic nervous system plays a vital role in respiration, digestion, circulation of blood and the activity of glands of internal and external secretion. Increased control over the automatic nervous system is common in hypnosis, it is responsible for many striking psychosomatic phenomenon. This system is primarily reflexive, controlling and regulating bodily functions which require no cooperation and of consciousness or intellect; yet it is not fully involuntary, as it is continual; almost constantly influenced by two related types of experience, namely by emotion and suggestion.

AUTO-SUGGESTION: (Not the same as Auto-Hypnosis) Suggestions made to oneself. It may be a product of wistful thinking or, more rationally, of self- persuasion; such as, self- talk or the way we speak to ourselves in our inner most minds.

BRAID, JAMES (1795-1860): Manchester, UK Physician, author "Neurohypnology" (1843), who discovered that so called "animal magnetism" had actually nothing to do with any magnetic influence and consequently gave modern name to the science of hypnotism. He used, at first, the method of fascination, but later turned to verbal suggestion. Among other things, he availed himself of hypnosis to perform painless surgical operations. "The state of hypnosis is essentially a state of mental concentration in which the faculties of the mind of the CLIENT are so engrossed with a single idea or train of thought as to be dead on indifferent to all other considerations and influences" J. Churchhill.

CATALEPSY: A form of high suggestibility, where the CLIENT manifests rigidity of the limbs and can be "molded" by putting him.her in various positions.

CHEVREUL PENDULUM: A portable contraption, originally designed by M. Chevruel involving a pendulum (a weight suspended by a string about 15 inches long) swaying over a cardboard card or piece of paper on which two lines are drawn crossing at right angles. (dividing the circle into quadrants) It is sometimes used to determine and increase client suggestibility or one's own power of concentration.

CONDITION, TO: To establish a learned, or "conditioned" emotion, response or reflex.

CONSCIOUS LEVEL: The normal awakening state of mind.

COUNTER SUGGESTION: A suggestion offered to an individual to challenge his fixed ideas concerning something or to inhibit the affect of a previous belief.

DANGERS OF HYPNOSIS: A client of good moral character will not accept any suggestion under hypnosis that is in conflict with his moral convictions. The harm resulting from hypnotism is infinitesimal compared with the good it has accomplished. In fact, no art ever practiced has so little evil to be responsible for, either through intend or accident.

DETACHMENT: When the CLIENT is aware of his environment, but does not participate or care to participate.

DREAM, HYPNOTIC: A dream suggested by the hypnotist, whatever the purpose. i.e., imagery, visualizations.

DREAM, RECALL: Dream recall is always better in the hypnotic state than in the waking state.

DURATION: A measured or estimated period of time. In the state of hypnosis, it may be unrealistically lengthened or shortened.

EIDETIC IMAGERY: Sensory imaginary, primarily visual, which practically reaches the clarity of actual perception. It is fairly common in children and extremely rare in adults, but can be readily aroused in hypnosis.

ESDAILE, JAMES: Edinburgh doctor who, having heard while in Calcutta, of the anesthetic use of hypnosis, turned it "to relieve the pain of a Hindu convict who was about to undergo a painful operation." Within several months, he reported 75 successful and painless major operations and several thousand minor operations with uniformly painless results. This included nineteen amputations.

FASCINATION: The method of hypnotizing by the fixation of eyes on a small shining object held slightly above the client's eyes. The method was introduced by James Braid. It is now usually combined with verbal suggestion.

FIXATION: Concentration of the attention on a single sensation or object.

FRACTIONATION: A good method of deepening the state of hypnosis, by hypnotizing, having the client open eyes but, not emerging, and hypnotizing again. This modulation of level of depth can be done in a variety of ways, with the eyes being the most common.

HALLUCINATION: A sensory experience arising quite apart from corresponding external stimulation. It is usually an indication of psychosis, and delirium or drug addiction, but it can be produced as a test of hypnotic depth in perfectly normal people.

HALLUCINATION, NEGATIVE: Strictly speaking it is not a hall-ucination, for it refers to failure to observe realities, such as a door or a sound of a whistle, Nevertheless, this effect can be readily produced in persons in hypnosis. It is a kind of suggested inability to see or hear certain things. They do not see something that is there.

HALLUCINATIONS, POSITIVE: When one can see an object that does not exist or alters the reality of something that is there..

HAND CLASPING TEST: Is a suggestibility test and it can also be used as induction. The client is asked to look straight into the hypnotist's eye while interlocking the fingers both hands and pressing them tightly together. Then he is told that he cannot separate them, and if the client is indeed unable to do so until the hypnotist commands him, he is regarded as ready for the proper treatment or else another experiment.

HANGOVER: A headache, drowsiness or nausea created by bringing the client out of hypnosis improperly…most often too fast, (Like standing up too fast creates a light-headedness) Drowsiness commonly following the first induction of a client never experiencing hypnosis previously.

HETERO-HYPNOSIS: Hypnosis produced by a second party.

HYPER-SUGGESTIBILITY: Heightened suggestibility characterized by deep hypnosis.

HYPER-SUGGESTIBILITY, HOMACTIVE: Marked increase in suggestibility caused by each preceding hypnotic session in, so far as the same procedure is followed.

HYPNO-ANALYSIS: Analyzing client's problem using hypnotic techniques while the client is in hypnotic state.

HYPNODIAL: A very light state of hypnosis.

HYPNOLOGY: The study of hypnosis.

HYPNOTIC STATE: The by-pass of the critical factor of the subconscious mind and establishment of selective acceptable thinking. (Dave Elman)

HYPNOTIST: The person conducting scientific experiments or aiding in wellbeing by means of hypnosis. Being a hypnotist is a specialist's job.

IDEO-MOTOR: Involuntary movement of muscles produced by suggestion.

IDEO-SENSORY: Pertaining to and affecting the senses.

INDUCTION: The process of technique of hypnotizing the client.

KINESIS: Physical movement.

KINESTHETIC: Muscles, tendons and organs stimulated by bodily movement.

LETHAGY: A state of hypnosis characterized by muscular flaccidity.

MESMERISM: The technique of hypnotizing developed by F.A. Mesmer in accordance with history of animal magnetism.

MIMICRY, UNCONSCIOUS: Involuntary activities of the client, particularly in the facial expression, reflecting the mental contents of the moment.

MONOIDEISM: James Braid's finding that the state of hypnosis depends on the narrowing or limiting of the clients attention. Setting 'focus'.

OBSESSION: A driving, sometimes irresistible idea; when combined with an emotion, it is likely to result inaction, sometimes endlessly repeated.

PHOBIA: Overwhelming fear of a fear felt previously.

POSTURAL SWAY TEST: A test of hypnotic readiness. The client is asked to stand, feet placed together, looking straight ahead staring fixedly at something slightly above the eyes, while the hypnotist stands squarely behind and begins to rock him/her slightly. Then the hypnotist tells the client that s/he feels he is being strongly drawn backwards. When the client loses his balance, he is caught by the supporting hands of the hypnotist. Not recommended due to safely issues!

POST-HYPNOTIC SUGGESTION: Something suggested to the client by the hypnotist, which is to be followed after the hypnotic state.

PYRAMIDING: Same as fractionation except the client is not emerged.

PSYCHOSOMATIC: Pertaining to bodily changes stimulated or depressed through mental influence.

RAPPORT: Working relationship between the hypnotist and his client.

RELAXATION PROGRESSIVE: Training how to relax increasingly by being subjected to repeated suggestions in a series of hypnotic sessions.

RESISTANCE: Some clients are unwilling to be hypnotized, for reasons of their own, even after they have given consent to that effect. In extreme cases, they may even break the hypnotic state. It is an inhibition or fear existing in the client of either the hypnotic state or the therapist.

SEAL: A hypnotic block, produced by telling the client no one else can hypnotize him, or until a certain signal is given.

SELECTIVE AMNESIA: Amnesia confined to a specific area of experience.

SOMNAMBULISM:

I.   Sleep-walking. This is a condition in which the individual is walking in his dream and even performing fairy complex tasks while being, for all practical purposes, asleep.

II. Deep hypnosis—in this state the eyes may be opened without waking, complete amnesia may result; positive and negative hallucinations may be induced. There are somnambules who sleep with open eyes; experience has proven that these are somnambulists by nature.

SUBCONSCIOUSNESS: The state in which mental processes, and possibly the resulting behavior, take apart from one's conscious awareness.

SUGGESTIBILITY: Susceptibility to suggestion.

SUGGESTION: A hint, proposal, offer or a new or alternative idea given in the waking state or otherwise. In hypnosis, it is a technique of influencing a client or of modifying his behavior. Whatever suggestion has done, suggestion can undo.

SUGGESTION, THERAPEUTIC: Suggestion aiming at the restoration of someone's health or serving some purpose of medical treatment.

SUGGESTION, POST-HYPNOTIC: Suggestion given by a hypnotist to his client to be subsequently carried out in the waking or conscious awareness state.

SUGGESTION, WAKING: Any theory of suggestion must take into account waking suggestion equally with hypnotic suggestion.

UNCONSCIOUS: Lack of consciousness. Unaware of all senses.

APPENDIX 2
RESOURCES

a. BIBLIOGRAPHY

Anne Bozzuto, R.N., BSN, MA and Thomas M. Bozzuto, D.O., D.I. Hom., "Homeopathy, Herbs and Hypnosis: Common Practices in Complementary and Alternative Medicine," *Jacksonville Medicine* (January 2000): 17.

Bandler Ricgard and Grinder John "The **Structure of Magic**, Vol. 1: A Book About Language and Therapy" Science and Behavior Books (1989)

Cornelia Kean, "Hypnosis: Neglected Weapon Against Chronic Pain? Overlooked, Inexpensive and Safe Modality Deserves Renewed Attention, According to Experts," *Pain Medicine News* 7:05 (May 2009.)

Edward B. Blanchard, Frank Andrasik, Tim A. Ahles, Steven J. Teders, and Dennis O'Keefe, "Migraine and Tension Headache: A Meta-Analytic Review, *"Behavior Therapy* 11:5 (November 1980): 613-631.

Elkins G, Jensen MP, Patterson DR. Hypnotherapy for the management of chronic pain. *Int J Clin Exp Hypn.* 2007;55:275-287.

Elman Dave, "Hypnotherapy" Westwood Publishing (1964)

Hartland, "Medical and Dental Hypnosis", 4th Editon, Churchill Livingstone, 2007

Hull, C. L. "Hypnosis and suggestibility: an experimental approach." Crown House Publishing. (1933/2002).

Jack Gerschman, B.D.Sc., L.D.S., Graham Burrows, M.D., Ch.B., B.Sc., M.D., D.P.M., F.R.A.C.N.Z.C.P. and Peter Reade, M.D.S., Ph.D.(Adel.), M.D.Sc., F.D.S.R.C.S., M.R.C.Path, "Hypnotherapy in the Treatment of Oro-Facial Pain," *Australian Dental Journal* 43:6 (December 1978): 492-496.

Jeremy Shulman, D.D.S., M.S., "Teaching Patients How to Stop Bruxing Habits," *The Journal of the American Dental Association* 132 (September 2001): 1275-1277.

J. H. Clarke and P. J. Reynolds, "Suggestive Hypnotherapy for Nocturnal Bruxism: A Pilot Study," *American Journal of Clinical Hypnosis,* 33:4 (April 1991): 251-253.

Karen Olness, M.D., "Helping Children and Adults with Hypnosis and Biofeedback," *Cleveland Clinic Journal of Medicine,* 75:2 (March 2008): S39.

Michael A. Gow, "Hypnosis with a 31-Year-Old Female with Dental Phobia Requiring an Emergency Extraction," *Contemporary Hypnosis,* 23(2) (2006): 83-91.

Michael B. LaCrosse, "Understanding Change: Five-Year Follow-up of Brief Hypnotic Treatment of Chronic Bruxism," *American Journal of Clinical Hypnosis* 36:4 (April 1994): 277-279.

Robert E. Rada, D.D.S., M.B.A and Charmaine Johnson-Leong, B.D.S., M.B.A. *"Stress, Burnout, Anxiety and Depression among Dentists"* J Am Dent Assoc, Vol 135, No 6, 788-794. (2004) American Dental Association

Roger E. Alexander, D.D.S.,"Stress Related Suicide by Dentists and Other Health Care Workers: Fact or Folklore" (*Journal of the American Dental Association June 2001*)

Scott DJ, Stohler CS, Egnatuk CM, et al. Placebo and nocebo effects are defined by opposite opioid and dopaminergic responses. *Arch Gen Psychiatry.* 2008;65:220-231.

Stack Steven, *"Occupation and Suicide"* Social Sciences Quarterly 384. 392 (2001)

Ulf Berggren and Sven G. Carlsson, "A Psychophysiological Therapy for Dental Fear," *Behavior Research and Therapy* 22:5 (1984): 487-492.

Wahbeh H, Elsas SM, Oken BS. Mind-body interventions: applications in neurology. *Neurology.* 2008;70:2321-2328.

Whalley, M. G., Brooks, G. B. (2009). *Enhancement of suggestibility and imaginative ability with nitrous oxide. Journal of Psychopharmacology,* 203, 745-752.

2. RECOMMENDED HYPNOTHERAPY PRACTITIONERS WITH EXPERTISE IN HYPNODONTICS

** **Bold type** indicates hypnotherapists who have contributed to this book with case histories and articles.

AUSTRALIA

**Christina Richards BA, MSc, MNLP, CH
hypnocounsellor@gmail.com

Mandy Moore CHt
mandy@livinghypnosis.com.au

CANADA

**Rev. Timothy Jones, B.Min., C.I., BCH, FNGH
Trinity Hypnotherapy,
Mississauga, Ontario. Canada.
www.trinityhypnotherapy.ca
Tel: 416-829-4161

GREAT BRITAIN

Josephine P Teague
MSc BSC, DipPsych., PGCE PGDHP AccHypSup CertHypEd
CertHypSup PNLP PDipNLP
24 Milton Road
Impington, Cambridge CB24 9NF   www.hypnosisandhealth.org.uk
j.teague@ntlworld.com
Tel: (01223) 235127

**Fiona Vitel, CHt, PNLP
2 Abbey House, High Street,
Winchcombe, Cheltenham GL54 5LT,
Gloucestershire
https://uk.linkedin.com/pub/fiona-vitel/6/525/286
Tel: +44 (0)1242 603505
Mobile: +44 (0)17514215871

LEBANON

Mona Santl BCH, C.I., MNLP
Mind Your Power, Hamra Street, Beirut
www.mindyourpower.com

Rita Baki MA, MNLP, CH
Visiting expert hypnotist
www.changeassociates.ae
rita@changeassociates.ae

NETHERLANDS

**Dr. Ina Oostrom,
Krommebeemd 56 ,
4907 DT Oosterhout.
www.HypnoseMentor.nl
Tel: 0031-162-455053

SPAIN

Beryl Comar MA, MEd, MNLP, BCH, CI., DipTEFLA
#1 Urb Palmeria, Orba, Denia,
Costa Blanca North
www.HypnoDontics.us
berylcomar@gmail.com

UNITED ARAB EMIRATES

**Beryl Comar MA, MEd, MNLP, BCH, CI., DipTEFLA
The Change Associates,
Block 2B, Knowledge Village, Dubai
www.HypnoDontics.us
www.changeassociates.ae
berylcomar@gmail.com
Tel: 00971 4 3902217 & 00971506554523

Rita Baki MA, MNLP, CH
The Change Associates,
Block 2B, Knowledge Village, Dubai
www.changeassociates.ae
rita@changeassociates.ae
Tel: 00971 50 41 88020

SWITZERLAND
** Nicole Wackernagel-Holzer
Poststrasse 13   Wil 9500
St Gallen, Switzerland
+41 79 820 2067
wackernagel@hypnosecenter.net
www.vita-libera.ch

UNITED STATES OF AMERICA
National Guild of Hypnotists,
Merrimack, New Hampshire - For names of up to date consulting
hypnotists in your area
www.ngh.net

**Seth-Deborah Roth CRNA, BA, CCHt, CI
20990 Redwood Road
Castro Valley, CA 94546
www.HypnotherapyForHealth.com
sethdeborah@HypnotherapyForHealth.com
Tel: 001 510.690.0699

**Elizabeth Campbell BCH CI
Center for Hypnosis of the Treasure Coast
611 S. Federal Highway, Suite K-1
Stuart, Florida 34994
www.elcHypnotherapy.comm
bethcamp00@yahoo.com
Tel: 772-419-8007

**Karen E. Lockman   CH
Fremont CA
Klockman@comcast.net
Tel: 510.792.2003

**Cheryl J Elman
Henderson, NC 27537
www.DaveElmanHypnosisInstitute.com
DaveElmanHypnosis@gmail.com
Tel: 252-432-2205

Cal Banyan MA. BCH. CI
Tustin, CA
www.HypnosisCenter.com   www.BanyanHypnosisCenter.com
Tel: 714.258.8380

Bob Brenner BCH
1707 Moncks Corner, The Villages, FL 32162
www.BrennerHypnosis.com   www.UnlockingMinds.com
bob@unlockingminds.com
Tel: 386.740.8224 / 407.333.9033

**Judy McBride CH
Annapolis MD
www.judymcbridehypnosis.com
Judy.mcb@verizon.com
Tel: 410.757.2576

**Helga Rahn   CH
Rochester NY
www.innerharmonyhypnosis.com
Tel: 585.662.9665

3. RECOMMENDED TRAINING IN HYPNOSIS/HYPNOTHERAPY

** Bold type indicates hypnotherapists who have contributed to this book with case histories and articles.

CANADA
**Rev. Timothy Jones, B.Min., M.Ht,. C.I., BCH, FNGH
Board Certified Consulting Hypnotherapist
Trinity Hypnotherapy, Mississauga, ON. CA.
Tel: 416-829-4161
www.trinityhypnotherapy.ca

**Ines Simpson
British Columbia, CA
advancedhypnosis.ca@gmail.com

GERMANY & SWITZERLAND
**Hansruedi Wipf
Hypnosecenter HYPNOSE.NET GmbH | Hansruedi Wipf
Poststrasse 2 | CH-8307 Effretikon
Telefon +41 79 261 78 42
wipf@hypnose.net www.hypnose.net

GREAT BRITAIN
Ursula James
10 Southwick Mews, London, W2 1JG
Tel: 0845 054 2460
www.HypnoDontics.co.uk
enquiries@HypnoDontics.co.uk

LEBANON
Mona Santl BCH, C.I., MNLP
Mind Your Power
Hamra Street, Beirut
www.mindyourpower.com

SPAIN
**Beryl Comar MA, MEd, MNLP, BCH, CI., DipTEFLA
#1 Urb Palmeria,
Orba, Nr Denia,
Costa Blanca North
www.HypnoDontics.us

berylcomar@gmail.com
Facebook: HypnoDontics

UNITED ARAB EMIRATES
**Beryl Comar MA, MEd, MNLP, BCH, Cl., DipTEFLA
The Change Associates,
Block 2B, Knowledge Village, Dubai.
Tel: 00971 4 3902217
www.HypnoDontics.us
www.changeassociates.ae
berylcomar@gmail.com

UNITES STATES OF AMERICA
**Gerald Kein
OmniHypnosis, 2607 S. Woodland Blvd,
DeLand, FL 32720
Tel: 001 877 525-2209
Tel: 001 386-738-9188
www.omnihypnosis.com
www.omnihypnosis.net
omnihypnosis@gmail.com

**Cheryl & H Larry Elman
Dave Elman Hypnosis Institute
920 Barker Rd
Henderson, NC 27537
Tel: 001 252-432-2205
www.DaveElmanHypnosisInstitute.com
DaveElmanHypnosis@gmail.com

National Guild of Hypnotists,
Merrimack, New Hampshire
www.ngh.net
For names of up to date consulting hypnotists in your area

4. RECOMMENDED SPECIALIST TRAINING IN HYPNOSIS FOR DENTISTS

Rev. Timothy Jones, B.Min., C.I., BCH, FNGH
Trinity Hypnotherapy,
Mississauga, Ontario. Canada.
www.trinityhypnotherapy.ca
Tel: 416-829-4161

Rev. Jones offers a 2-day *Introduction to HypnoDontics* course for which dentists can earn CEU's with their College under Ontario Regulation 27/10, s. 3 (4) of the Dentistry Act (1991).

Beryl Comar MA, MEd, MNLP, CI., DipTEFLA
The Change Associates,
Block 2B, Knowledge Village, Dubai, UAE.

Beryl Comar #1 Urb Palmeria, Orba, Alicante, Spain
www.HypnoDontics.us
www.changeassociates.ae
berylcomar@gmail.com
Tel: 00971 4 3902217 & 0034
Skype: berylcomar

Beryl teaches 2-day *Introduction to HypnoDontics* certified course. Both dentists and hypnotists may apply for CEU's with their licensing body. This course is available in-house and at locations around the Middle East and Europe. Beryl is available to speak and/or train at your location and train at your Hypnosis Convention or Dental Convocation worldwide.

Beryl has been awarded at international level by National Guild of Hypnotists and National Federation of NeuroLinguistic Programming and taught the first NLP and Hypnotherapy courses in the Middle East beginning 2001

Dr. John Butler MBSH, CHT MA, BA (Hons.), BSc (Hons.), DHP,
Dip. A.T., FNRHP
The Institute of Hypnotherapy for Medical and Dental Practice,
37 Orbain Road, Fulham, London SW6 7JZ
www.ihmdp.org and info@ihmdp.org
Tel: 00 44 (0) 207 385 1166

Dr Butler wrote and trained the first official training in hypnotherapy in
the NHS in 1992. Hypnosis has been endorsed by the BMA: 1892,
1955, and 1982. He taught at the Royal College of Nursing in London
and internationally. IHMDP offers certified courses on HypnoDontics:
Foundation and Advanced - for dentists and dental care professionals.

American Society of Clinical Hypnosis
140 N. Bloomingdale Rd.
Bloomingdale, IL 60108-1017
(630/980-4740)

ASCH offers training and credentials for licensed health care
professionals. The ASCH Certification and Approved Consultant
Program has become a standard for hypnosis practice in the US and
requires advanced training in Dentistry and hypnosis from accredited
institutions.

American Board of Medical Hypnosis www.abmedhyp.net

ABMH provides hypnotist certification for physicians.

Society for Clinical & Experimental Hypnosis
P.O. Box 252
Southborough, MA 01172
(508) 598-5553
www.sceh.us

The American Society of Clinical Hypnosis and The Society of Clinical
and Experimental Hypnosis (SCEH) accepts certification from ABMH,
which is considered to be the highest credential in medical hypnosis,
but one of the requirements for certification is at least five years of
clinical hypnosis experience in practice.

International Medical and Dental Hypnotherapy Association (IMDHA)
Rural Route #2 Box 2468
Laceyville, PA 18623
(570) 869-1021
www.imdha.com

IMDHA focused on Hypnosis and Health Care since 1986. Members cross a broad range of professions.

IMDHA Practitioners work harmoniously with allied healthcare professionals to aid individuals in dealing with specific challenges and procedures.

Author's Bio - Beryl Comar BEd., MEd., MA, MNLP, CI

With a deep interest in hypnosis and transcendental meditation, and following a successful tour as teacher of English in Tanzania, Beryl visited Dubai (United Arab Emirates) in 1976 for a job interview, and stayed. Her consequent career as School Principal, College Lecturer and Head of Dept at a Women's University meant long summer holidays and the opportunity to travel around the world five times. Beryl founded TESOL Arabia which is now the largest TESOL group in the world.

After taking a year off to study for a Masters Degree in Applied Linguistics at Reading University UK, in 1984 she returned to Dubai with a fascination for NLP and desire to further study Hypnotherapy. NLP studies with Richard Bandler in Mexico and India; Wil Horton in USA, Malaysia and India; and advanced hypnosis courses with Gerald Kein and the National Guild of Hypnotists. led to her leaving academia in 1995. She set up the first NLP and Hypnosis Coaching and Training Institute in the Middle East in Dubai. People said she was "crazy, it would never take off or be accepted!"

Now, Beryl Comar has established herself as the Obvious Expert in Emotional Intelligence, Hypnotherapy, NLP and EFT in the Middle East, and a leading authority in communication skills, Clinical and NeuroLinguistic Hypnotherapy and trained hundreds of coaches and hypnotists now practicing around the world. She has helped many expats and Emiratis, with issues from fears and phobias, to smoking cessation and eating disorders. Her expertise includes confidence and esteem building for individuals, as well as motivation training within corporations, pain management in clinics and leadership skills in banks and hotels. Since 2012, Beryl has been increasingly involved in dental and medical work - pain management, hypnosis for dentistry, hypnofertility, gender issues, and hypnobirthing. Referrals from doctors and previous clients have built the bulk of her business.

Beryl puts lots of energy and empathy into her sessions and workshops, to ensure they are practical and informative, as well as entertaining and fun. She often speaks at international conferences. Beryl has been awarded the following by the National Guild of Hypnotists: The Hallmark Award 2014, Member of the Order of the Braid 2010, and the Outstanding Presentation 2007. The National Federation of NLP has presented Beryl their highest awards as trainer and presenter. Her students and clients have included royalty, members of government, CEOs and Olympic sportsmen. For three years she trained Dubai Police in NeuroLinguistic Programming (NLP), and Dubai Electricity and Water (DEWA) in Emotional Intelligence.
Beryl is available to speak at your conferences and workshops.

"We enjoyed your half-day workshop very much. Thanks for making it so lively! Many of my colleagues told me they benefited a lot even though it was a short session. The materials were relevant and straight to the point. I can't wait to get started with real clients. It was even worth waking up early at weekends!"

"I feel confident to use hypnosis with the children that come to me for dental work. Thank you, this has been a very enlightening few days"